Implementing RTI Successfully in Your Middle/High School

Amy Carney-Heath, Heath Dudley, Jan Brown, Katie Preston

First Edition © 2010 First Steps Library

Published by First Steps Library
www.FirstStepsLibrary.com

All rights reserved. No part of this publication may be reproduced, stored in a retrieval system, or transmitted in any form or by any means, electronic, mechanical, photocopying, recording, or otherwise, without the prior written permission of the publisher and/or author.

AIMSweb. Copyright © 2008 NCS Pearson, Inc. Reproduced in black and white with permission. All rights reserved.

"AIMSweb" is a trademark, in the US and/or other countries, of Pearson Education, Inc. or its affiliates(s).

Printed in the United States of America

PUBLISHER CONTACT
First Steps Library
Flagship Enterprise Center
2701 Enterprise Drive
Box No. 213
Anderson IN, 46013

Photos for Chapter 6 taken by Anna Blankenbaker.

Edited by Lindsay Conner.

ISBN: 978-0-578-05662-3

DESIGN AND LAYOUT
Community Networks
www.CommunityNet.biz

WELCOME TO FIRST STEPS LIBRARY

The First Steps Library is a series of brief, practical tools which equip, empower, and encourage teachers along their journey of professional development.

The First Steps Library is created by teachers for teachers. Each book is about making connections with your children. Join us for your First Steps along the path of teaching excellence.

Please refer to our website, www.FirstStepsLibrary.com, for supplemental materials to support RtI in your school.

TABLE OF CONTENTS

Appreciation	9
Preface	11
Recollections & Reflections	13
Glossary	15

1   WHAT IS RTI?   **19**

Amy Carney-Heath
Reading Specialist & Teacher

2   RTI FROM THE PRINCIPAL'S PERSPECTIVE   **27**

Heath Dudley
School Principal

3   THE LEADERSHIP TEAM   **41**

Heath Dudley
School Principal

4   PROFESSIONAL DEVELOPMENT   **51**

Jan Brown
Special Education Teacher & Behavioral Consultant

Heath Dudley
School Principal

5	ASSESSMENT	**63**

Jan Brown
Special Education Teacher & Behavioral Consultant

6	RTI FROM A TEACHER'S PERSPECTIVE	**85**

Amy Carney-Heath
Reading Specialist & Teacher

7	SCHEDULING RTI	**105**

Katie Preston
School Counselor

8	FAMILY PARTNERSHIP	**113**

Katie Preston
School Counselor

9	CONCLUDING THOUGHTS	**121**

Amy Carney-Heath
Reading Specialist & Teacher

References	123
Additional Resources	129

Appendices	131
Appendix A	*132*
Appendix B	*134*
Appendix C	*136*
Appendix D	*137*
Appendix E	*138*
Appendix F	*140*
Appendix G	*141*
Appendix H	*142*
Appendix I	*144*
About the Authors	147

APPRECIATION

This book is dedicated to the teachers at Yorktown Middle School, Yorktown, Indiana. On a daily basis, these teachers strive to serve students and families. This fact was most evident through the implementation of RtI. We appreciated each teacher's strength, and we most appreciated your efforts to work together, to work beyond a normal school day, and to work out of your "comfort zone." Thank you for doing what is best for children. This book would not be possible without you.

PREFACE

Middle school reading instruction may be neglected in many middle schools, but that does not mean it cannot regain strength and prove its value. We cannot afford to relegate a high percentage of underachieving readers to the high school dropout pile. The statistics show that most of the drop outs have serious reading problems.

This is a time when over three million American middle-grades students who enter the ninth grade will not graduate in four years. Fewer than forty percent of young adults hold an associate's or bachelor's degree, and substantial racial and income gaps persist. According to labor market projections, by 2020, six of ten jobs will require a quality postsecondary degree or credential. Thus, reading proficiency is important for all middle school students.

Prior to the establishment of middle schools, most elementary schools contained kindergarten through eighth grade students. Most elementary schools at that time had an eight period day for sixth through eighth grade students with one period for English and one period for reading. Most middle schools dropped reading classes, and thus reading teachers, and combined English and reading into language arts classes. They did this to reduce the number of periods and provide more time per period or to add other content. Now middle schools need to reexamine their priorities and consider new ways to upgrade the reading proficiency of all their students.

In this book, the authors focus on the critical relationship of Response to Instruction (RtI) and multi-tiered instruction in regards to middle grades reading. In this system, a focus is placed on school-wide reading activities to build strong middle grades readers. The tiered instruction approach is used in addition to a required reading course for all students.

Superintendents, middle/high school principals, counselors, school librarians, teachers, directors of special education, curriculum specialists, and college professors will appreciate the complete coverage in this book on the steps needed to establish a multi-tiered reading program from the perspective of various school personnel. This also addresses the search for and use of appropriate assessment and instructional materials, schedule changes, and the use of data to communicate with families and the community.

As states move to common academic standards that include reading test for grades 3-8, *Implementing RTI Successfully in Your Middle/High School* is a timely and comprehensive look at how middle/high schools can increase reading achievement for ALL students.

Dr. Jack W. Humphrey
Middle Grades Reading Network
University of Evansville

RECOLLECTIONS & REFLECTIONS

As you and your colleagues begin to explore RtI as described in this text, you will embark upon a personal journey that may challenge your thinking, your beliefs, and your attitudes. It's not going to be enough for you to know the reasoning behind the RtI requirement and the research that led to it – or to agree with what the authors say. The real challenge will be acting on what you learn – having your instruction reflect your evolving beliefs. Habits are tough to break, and change is not always our friend. But, being a teacher means being a life-long learner, setting goals, and constantly being reflective in your teaching. For individuals who embrace this reality, learning becomes more of a gift than a chore.

So when you read through this text, we encourage you to engage in gathering your Recollections & Reflections. Using this R & R activity should guide you to clarify ideas and jot down important points that you want to remember. Listed below is a series of prompts designed to help you recollect and reflect on ideas in each chapter. Have fun with them, and, who knows, someone's R & Rs might just spark a great conversation or an even greater idea!

After you finish the chapter, close the book and write down 3 words or phrases that immediately come to mind.

- Write down two helpful pieces of information you learned.

- Write down one question that you still have.

- Write down one way that this chapter has changed your thinking about RtI.

- Write down any ideas you have for how you might implement something from this chapter.

- Write down a significant "ah-ha" moment you experienced while reading this chapter (if any).

- Describe something from your professional experience that came to mind as you worked with the ideas in this chapter.

- Write down any resources from the chapter, your discussions, or personal web surfing that would help in implementing RtI in your school.

- Is the goal that you identified at the beginning of this experience still the same? If not, explain why it changed and then write down your new goal.

GLOSSARY

Accelerated Reader (AR): Reading management program in which students select books to read, take computerized quizzes to check reading comprehension, and receive immediate feedback. This may help students gain confidence in reading and become self-motivated readers.

Aimline: Line graph depicting a student's progress toward a benchmark.

Alignment: The concept of assessing what you are teaching and teaching what you are assessing.

Brain Gym: Program which incorporates movement to enhance whole-brain learning.

Decoding: Word identification as determined by Dynamic Indicators of Basic Early Literacy Skills (DIBELS) assessment.

DIBELS: Assessment which provides teachers and principals with a means to gauge progress toward benchmark goals in order to determine reading success. Stands for Dynamic Indicators of Basic Early Literacy Skills.

Executive Functioning Skills (EF Skills): A set of cognitive abilities that controls and regulates other abilities and behaviors and is necessary for goal-directed behavior.

Fidelity: Measurement of precision, faithfulness, and accuracy in assessment and instruction across the environment.

Intervention: Instruction in an identified area of need that supplements or intensifies classroom curriculum.

ISTEP+: Test that assesses students' knowledge and ability in core subjects at each grade level. Stands for The Indiana Statewide Testing for Educational Progress-Plus.

IDEA: Law which determines how intervention services are provided for children with disabilities. Stands for The Individuals with Disabilities Education Act.

Lexile: Measurement of how difficult it is for a reader to take meaning from a text.

MAZE Test: Assessment used to test comprehension skills in reading by utilizing words deleted from a passage and choices for the deleted words.

Oral reading fluency: The speed at which a student can read orally.

Probes: Brief assessments of academic progress.

Progress monitoring: The act of measuring performance over time to determine effectiveness of intervention.

RtI and Multi-tiered Instruction: Educational reform terms used interchangeably in different states. The Indiana Department of Instruction defines RtI as a "framework for prevention, advancement and early intervention which involves determining whether ALL students are learning and progressing optimally academically and behaviorally when provided with high-quality instruction." (IDEA, 2009).

STAR Test: Assessment designed to help find a student's independent reading level.

Universal screen: School-wide assessment of age-appropriate, critical academic skills to determine risk, high ability, or both.

ZPD level: The reading-level range from which a student should be selecting books for optimal growth in reading without frustration.

CHAPTER ONE
WHAT IS RTI?

Amy Carney-Heath
Reading Specialist & Teacher

"To me, Interventions and Extensions class helped me a lot. I have never finished a book by myself because I don't like to read. I came from China, so I have had to learn to talk all over again, or I can't have a conversation with anyone. Learning to read a book is a helpful way to learn how to speak English."

– Eighth Grade Boy

The Definition of RtI

Response to Instruction (RtI) has many definitions. The Individuals with Disabilities Education Improvement Act defines RtI "... as a method for identifying students who will profit from differentiated and appropriate instruction in the classroom" (IDEA, 2004). The International Reading Association (IRA, 2005) defines RtI as "... a coherent instructional plan that provides coordinated reading lessons every day for every student at every level of intervention" (IRA, 2009). The RtI Action Network Online Forum defined RtI as a "framework for school and student improvement" (Casey, Elliot, & Prasse, 2008). A Colorado Springs

High School defined RtI as "an instructional model that links lessons, or 'interventions,' of increasing intensity with frequent monitoring of student progress...." (Samuels, 2009). The Indiana Department of Instruction defines RtI as a "framework for prevention, advancement and early intervention which involves determining whether all students are learning and progressing optimally academically and behaviorally when provided with high-quality instruction" (IDEA, 2009). Our international and national agencies, our 50 states, and even our corporations within the state of Indiana differ in their definitions of RtI. Even so, the international and national educational audiences agree that education must change, and the agent of change is RtI. *Education must systematically advance individual student achievement through matching assessment with curriculum while utilizing tiered instructional models.*

Our school, Yorktown Middle School (YMS), continues to define RtI as we learn about the RtI model and how to implement the model in our school. Because we serve students in an Indiana public school system, our definition aligns with our state's vision:

- To create teacher leaders (see chapters 2 and 3),
- To offer professional development opportunities (see chapter 4),
- To assess and progress monitor and to engage in a data-based decision making progress (see chapter 5),
- To offer intervention or extension opportunities (see chapter 6),
- To create a master schedule (see chapter 7), and
- To partner with families for the achievement of individual students (see chapter 8).

In addition, our school utilizes varied international and national definitions to inform our process in order to create a program that is both teacher-friendly and student-centered. *Here at YMS, we desire our program to outlast the acronym RtI.* We desire to create a multi-tiered, instructional model that focuses on our individual student's achievement goals. We also desire to create a model that will inspire other middle schools and high schools struggling with the concept of implementing a curriculum to meet the needs of all learners.

Achievement-Centered Multi-Tiered Instruction

RtI focuses on the creation of a building-wide, multi-tiered approach to instruction. Educators focus on student progress, not student labels (Casey, Elliot, & Prasse, 2008). Educators are concerned with how students receive quality core instruction, as well as how to document student achievement. If students are not meeting grade level benchmarks and goals, they are offered a scientific, research-based intervention opportunity (IDEA, 2004). If students exceed grade level expectations, they receive extension services. RtI meets the needs of all learners through a systematic process (IDOE, 2009).

The Basic Components of a Multi-Tiered Instructional Approach

The basic components of RtI include: 1) a universal screening process, 2) a student progress monitoring system, and 3) data-based decision-making procedures (IDEA, 2004, & IDOE, 2009). Through this process, educators are assessing all students for academic excellence or academic risk (IDOE, 2009).

After a universal screening process is administered, an RtI Team reviews the results, makes decisions about student placement, and assigns each student with the appropriate teacher. The team explains the results to the classroom teachers, and the classroom teachers explain the results to individual students. At this point, the RtI team has tiered instruction for individual students and has grouped students into flexible learning groups (Tomlinson, 2005). Through this process, teachers see students as individual learners and endeavor to meet the unique needs of the individual learner.

The Framework for a Multi-Tiered Instructional Approach

"RtI is not a program or curriculum; rather (RtI is) a systems approach to enhancing the capacity of schools" (Casey, Elliot, & Prasse, 2008). The framework of a multi-tiered instructional approach balances research-based core curriculum with instruction. Our RtI Team examines the core curriculum of individual students through unit benchmark tests. Teachers enter benchmark test scores into our online grading system. If students are not on grade level, they are failing benchmark tests and are not meeting the AIMS line of the universal screener, as predetermined by our school psychologist. This flags the student, prompting our team to examine the student's state test scores and ZPD levels; depending on the ZPD level, the reading specialist may administer a running record assessment (Clay, 2000). If the student is exceeding grade-level expectations on benchmark assessments in reading, science, or math, the student is placed in one of more of the classes: Advanced Language Arts, Biology, or Algebra. In addition, at the end of the day, the student takes an Extensions

CHAPTER ONE

class with an advanced science component or advanced reading component. The RtI framework is a problem-solving process (IDOE, 2009, IDEA, 2004, Palenchar & Boyer, 2008, and Samuels, 2009). The RtI team first defines the student's problem in order to determine whether the student needs intervention or an extension. Then, the RtI team evaluates the student's progress and addresses the student's needs in a positive way.

Through the RtI framework, the RtI team and school faculty are offering differentiated instruction through three tiers. Tier one students are responding to the core curriculum. Tier two students need an intervention in addition to the core curriculum. Tier three students need an intensive intervention in addition to the core curriculum and intervention. If a student responds to the intervention, the student moves to another tier; thus, the tiers allow for flexible grouping. If the student is not responding to an intervention, the RtI Team investigates why the student's needs are not being met. Tiered instruction meets the needs of all students in all subject areas. Our school as a whole tiers instruction, and individual teachers tier instruction based on student progress. An effective RtI model allows students to move within a tier or within a tiered classroom. Differentiated instruction is:

> "a process to approach teaching and learning for students of differing abilities in the same class. The intent is to maximize each student's growth where he or she is . . . rather than expecting students to modify themselves for the curriculum" (Hall, 2002).

RtI invites middle and high school teachers to respond on a higher level and no longer ignore reading with the excuse, "I am not a reading teacher." RtI asks faculties, not individual teachers, to respond to the growing needs of our students.

Quick Chapter Review

This chapter explains the following:

- The definition of RtI
- Achievement centered multi-tiered instruction
- The basic components of a multi-tiered instructional approach
- The framework for a multi-tiered instructional approach

RECOLLECTIONS & REFLECTIONS
Chapter 1: What is RtI?

1. After you finish the chapter, close the book and write down 3 words or phrases that immediately come to mind.

2. Write down two helpful pieces of information you learned.

3. Write down one question that you still have.

4. Write down one way that this chapter has changed your thinking about RtI.

5. Write down any ideas you have for how you might implement something from this chapter.

6. Write down a significant "ah-ha" moment you experienced while reading this chapter (if any).

7. Describe something from your professional experience that came to mind as you worked with the ideas in this chapter.

8. Write down any resources from the chapter, your discussions, or personal web surfing that would help in implementing RtI in your school.

9. Is the goal that you identified at the beginning of this experience still the same? If not, explain why it changed and then write down your new goal.

CHAPTER TWO
RTI FROM THE PRINCIPAL'S PERSPECTIVE

Heath Dudley
School Principal

"My Interventions and Extensions class has helped me in many ways. It helps me learn how to look at context clues, facts, and inferences. It also helps me improve my reading. It helps me read more and more every day. It is amazing!"

– Seventh Grade Girl

Getting Started

As a new principal in 2006, I began hearing the word "RtI" from our Special Education Director during routine administration meetings. Response to Instruction was described as a model that would become the alternative to the district's current discrepancy model that used a comparison of a child's IQ versus academic achievement to determine special education eligibility. The purpose would be to identify students earlier, ideally Kindergarten through second grade, in order to begin intervening with students who in the past may have been delayed or denied possible qualification until upper elementary or early middle school, using the

RtI Implementation Process

2006-2008

1. RtI became an alternative to special education's discrepancy model, with the purpose of identifying K-2 students for special education services.
   a. Researched how to implement RtI.
   b. Implemented STAR Reading and Math.
   c. Modified Block Schedule.

2008-2009

1. The special education director asked for benchmark data, documentation of intervention strategies, and implementation of programs based on recommendations.
   a. Presented RtI to staff and asked the staff to complete an interest inventory and determine if they would like to teach an intervention or extension class.
   b. Monitored STAR Data and created graphs of student progress.
   c. Revised schedule to an 8 period day.

2009-2010

1. The special education director helped the special education teacher and reading teacher secure teaching materials for RtI.
   a. Assigned teachers for intervention or extension classes.
   b. Continued to monitor STAR and implemented MAZE.
   c. Revised schedule to include Tier 1, 2, and 3 in an 8 period day.

figure 2.1

discrepancy model. As a new principal, much of this talk evolving around IDEA 2004, collecting unimaginable amounts of data, and conducting continuous progress monitoring was extremely intimidating and seemed like an enormously overwhelming task that lie ahead for our corporation. Honestly, I was happy that I was at the middle school, where it seemed there would not be as much focus and attention. Remember, I was serving in my first year as principal with only two years experience as an assistant principal. I could have never imagined what would occur within the next three years.

How the Ball Got Rolling

Through 2006 to 2008, I was involved in a great deal of discussions, planning sessions, and continued research regarding RtI (see figure 2.1). The focus still appeared to be squarely placed on our two elementary schools, with the greatest emphasis being placed on the primary grade building. As the process was first implemented in the elementary schools, we began to receive the normal amount of requests for testing for special education services from the parents of struggling students. However, around mid-year of the 2008-2009 school year, our Special Education director began asking us for our benchmark data on these students using research based assessments, and desired to collect core curriculum benchmark assessment data. Also, the director prompted us for documentation of the intervention strategies and programs that had been implemented with the student, prior to the recommendation of completing an educational evaluation for the purposes of special education. This process initiated the momentum we needed to get the process moving, with regards to Response to Instruction at Yorktown Middle School.

How Reading Comprehension Became our Target

The decision to attack reading comprehension as our first target area of tiered instruction was an easy choice, but the program evolved over many years. Between the years of 2004 and 2008, our building established a school improvement goal of "Writing Across the Curriculum." This was not a unique goal to Yorktown Middle School, as there were strong pushes to improve student writing skills in many corporations across the state of Indiana. With the great deal of emphasis that was placed on student responses on standardized tests, that were connected to school accountability initiatives, it made great sense for many schools to incorporate student writing initiatives into their PL 221 school improvement plans. At YMS, we developed consistent writing prompts throughout the subject areas, at each grade level, and developed a calendar when students would participate in these writing prompts. Following completion of each prompt, these writing samples were assessed, using a common rubric that our teachers created, integrating the 6 + 1 Writing Traits with the ISTEP+ assessment rubric. The official data from these scores were collected by our data team and used for our school improvement and accreditation efforts. In addition to the school-wide writing rubric, based on these traits, the 6 + 1 program was also a major piece of our improvement plan and was embedded into our classroom instruction. Professional development for the 6 + 1 Writing Traits has been ongoing and continues to this day for all teachers in our building.

CHAPTER TWO

During this same time frame, during the 2006-2007 school year, we were running a modified block schedule for our seventh and eighth grade students at Yorktown Middle School. The students participated in extended periods four days a week, Monday through Thursday, in the subject areas of Language Arts, Social Studies, Mathematics, and Science, meeting every other day in two of the four subjects. The schedule for Friday was the traditional seven-period schedule (with a homeroom included). However, during this same time frame, our corporation had begun assessing students' reading skills and math skills using the Renaissance programs, STAR reading and math, and Accelerated Reader and Math. As any administrator should always do, I am constantly observing what I see in classes, as well as data from assessment. I began observing two things: as a student at YMS, you could have a very different experience with regards to writing versus reading, depending upon your Language Arts teacher. I observed that teachers have their comfort levels and interest areas, and it is easy to focus on what you know or enjoy. This observation is not to say any state standards were ignored or failed to be covered, but it was readily apparent as to what each teacher's comfort area was. What I saw, particularly at the eighth grade level, was one teacher who favored the writing, grammar, and composition side of the Language Arts curriculum, while the other teacher at the eighth grade level focused more on literature, novels, and response to literature. Therefore, we were sending students to the high school with very different experiences one year prior to their freshmen year, when they would begin working for credits towards graduation. I wondered how this could impact that crucial first semester of the freshman year.

I began noticing, based on data from STAR and informal observations and conversations with our teachers, that we had many students not reading at the appropriate grade level. This caused issues in more than Language Arts classes. It created problems for students in Social Studies, Science, and Mathematics. Many of the textbooks used in schools are written at higher readability levels than the grade level for which they are intended. Therefore, if we have students reading below grade level, there was a definitive gap creating academic issues. In addition to these two areas of concern, there were three consecutive classes on the way from the elementary that were considerably larger than we could comfortably staff with the available teachers at Yorktown Middle School. This challenge led me to creatively find a way to add teachers to absorb the large class sizes and separate the Language Arts class into two separate courses, one for literature and reading and the other for writing. These were the first steps into effectively addressing reading at the middle school level. The tiered instruction approach, on top of adding a required reading course each year of middle school, has only strengthened the program and insured that fewer students are going to leave Yorktown Middle School with any type of gap in their reading abilities.

How RtI was Introduced to YMS Faculty and Students

In 2009, we introduced the Response to Instruction program to Yorktown Middle School. This program has been the most exciting, rewarding, challenging, and difficult initiative that I have ever been a part of as an administrator. To this very day, the journey continues to present new twists and turns as we learn during the infancy of our tiered instructional program. Our Response to Instruction team continues to focus its efforts on using established research and best practices during the implementation process; however, we continue to discover that there is not a great deal of middle-school-specific research. We hope that your school district will find elements within our program that will assist you in developing your own program. The purpose of this writing is to share our experiences of building this program in our school. Hopefully, you can draw from these experiences and generate ideas that might work in your building, or you may relate to mistakes we made and aim to avoid those during your implementation process. I think the most valuable lesson that I have learned during this entire process is that one "canned" method cannot work for every school. It is essential that you identify your school and district goals, with regards to tiered instruction, and then study how you can make your current situation work within defined parameters.

The Principal's Duties

Once your district identifies parameters, you can then begin moving ahead and always keep the momentum moving forward. In order to keep the process moving, you must analyze your philosophies as a leader and find the best ways to mesh your style into the implementation of your tiered instructional program. Regardless of your leadership style, I can assure you of three roles you will need to fill that will be essential in implementing RtI as an administrator:

1. You must play the role of cheerleader.

You should be prepared to be on the front line leading the charge about the positive impacts that a program such as RtI will have on your students' learning. You must also continually praise and applaud those who are willing to give the extra hours of work to make the program a success. You will have many people in your building working outside of their comfort levels, with regards to workloads and content. Continually letting them know the importance of their roles and your gratitude for this commitment often keeps them going when it would be very easy for them to throw up their arms and "throw in the towel." Common sense will also tell you that one administrator cannot coordinate and manage an effort such as this single-handedly. Regardless, there still must be that identification with your staff because you are the foundation of the program and a key player in the continual improvement of the program. If you aren't out front providing the leadership, you will quickly lose "buy in" and the program may lose momentum before it even gets off the ground.

Not only do you have to be a cheerleader to the staff within your building, but there is a certain amount of promotional work that must be done with students and their parents. Tiered instruction, with additional remediation, is a very foreign concept in most middle schools, where the focus is "reading to learn" rather than "learning to read." Therefore, removing an extended time to complete homework and assignments (that is, study hall) and replacing it with a time for "reading" was questioned by some parents and students to say the least. We all understand how overextended many of our families are with activities outside of school. Also, as you learn more about our program, you will understand that all of our students are participating in the tiered instruction program. Though students are not part of the intervention and remediation tiers, we had to convince students that dedicating time each day to read a high-interest book within their Zone of Proximal Development was also raising their skill level. This concept is a difficult "sell," particularly to seventh and eighth graders. I created a presentation and regularly traveled to each classroom to explain the program and answer student questions (see figure 2.2). I explained how we tied their Maze test scores to their Zone of Proximal Development (see Appendix A) to determine the tiered classes. I wanted the students to know that this type of program was unique for middle schools and would give them a great advantage for the remainder of their lives, if they utilized this time to improve their reading skills. I used analogies that would make sense to students (such as rehearsing dance routines, shooting free throws daily, or practicing a musical instrument) and compared them to reading. In all of these analogies, students made the connection that they very well may not participate in these activities for the remainder of their lives, but reading and processing information is the one skill from their educational career that will certainly remain relevant for their entire life. Therefore, effort and dedication to this practice should be taken as seriously as their interests outside of school. So get your pom-poms and go out and promote your program!

2. You must create teacher leaders.

As I mentioned in the above section, one person cannot solely control such a complex initiative as tiered instruction. There are so many different areas of expertise needed to make this program effective. In my opinion, there is not an administrator in existence that could fill all the roles, even if they chose to do so. Therefore, even if this is out of your comfort level as an admin-

Introducing RtI to Students

WHY RtI?

1. RtI (Response to Instruction) is a state and federal initiative. It is not optional.
2. We receive nothing for implementing this program, other than students becoming better readers.
3. Our focus is currently reading, but we will begin focusing on math, behavior, and other areas in the future.
4. Reading is a key to being successful in all academic areas and in life in general.
5. We are also working on brain functions, test taking, and basic executive skills.

IF YOUR COACH TOLD YOU? ...

1. *Shoot 20 free throws....* Would you say, "I shoot 150 at home on my own. I don't need to do that"?
2. *Use a lighter bat because the one you are swinging is too heavy....* Would you listen?
3. *Practice your band playing chart for 20 minutes during class....* Would you say, "I don't need to do that I practice an hour at home every night".
4. *Run 2 miles during practice....* Would you respond, "I don't need to do that. I run 3 every night".

figure 2.2

istrator, you should be prepared to relinquish a fair amount of the program's control to those you identify as your "core team" responsible for building your tiered instructional program. Once this core team is assembled, there must be an environment that allows the members to create, explore, and experiment with their own ideas and philosophies. As I mentioned previously, there is not a plethora of research involving the middle school level and tiered instruction. As you progress, mistakes will be made, new ideas will be developed, and research will be discovered that will cause you to adjust how you do things within the program. By not putting constraints on team members, it creates the freedom to "think outside the box" and create true teacher leaders, rather than members of a team responsible for a specific task. This has always been my core philosophy of leadership, even prior to the tiered instruction initiative, making it easy to foster this open and supportive environment for our core team.

3. You must fill the role of "handyman."

As an administrator, you should be prepared to do some things you have probably not done in recent years. The amount of work involved in implementing this program is mind numbing. And once it is implemented, maintaining and managing it is even more work. Analyzing data is one of the obvious responsibilities with which administrators feel comfortable. We have become so focused on using data to drive instruction, achievement, curriculum, and decision making that it is natural for us to offer our assistance in this area. However, because of the sheer amount of hours needed to make this program successful, I have found myself doing things this year that I have not done since leaving the classroom as a teacher. You may find yourself grading your student's benchmark assessment tests, administering benchmark or strategic progress monitoring assessments, and entering scores into your data management software. The bottom line: This initiative is going to take a great deal of human effort. You must be willing to become competent in the many facets of the program and offer your manpower when the time calls. I believe that monitoring this is not only a necessity, but it also strengthens the buy-in from the faculty, when they see the principal involved in the process, rather than a "trickle down" initiative that places all of the work on the teachers. Get your toolbox out and be ready to roll up your sleeves to be a part of the process!

Quick Chapter Review

This chapter explains the following:

- Getting started
- How the ball got rolling
- How reading comprehension became our target
- How RtI was introduced to faculty and students
- The principal's role

RECOLLECTIONS & REFLECTIONS
Chapter 2: RtI from the Principal's Perspective

1. After you finish the chapter, close the book and write down 3 words or phrases that immediately come to mind.

2. Write down two helpful pieces of information you learned.

3. Write down one question that you still have.

4. Write down one way that this chapter has changed your thinking about RtI.

5. Write down any ideas you have for how you might implement something from this chapter.

6. Write down a significant "ah-ha" moment you experienced while reading this chapter (if any).

7. Describe something from your professional experience that came to mind as you worked with the ideas in this chapter.

8. Write down any resources from the chapter, your discussions, or personal web surfing that would help in implementing RtI in your school.

9. Is the goal that you identified at the beginning of this experience still the same? If not, explain why it changed and then write down your new goal.

CHAPTER THREE
THE LEADERSHIP TEAM

Heath Dudley
Principal

"In my Interventions and Extensions class, I have learned a few things. I have noticed that my reading level sky-rocketed. I am reading at a much higher level now. My teachers are continuing to help me, and they are doing a good job at it."

– Seventh Grade Girl

How to Consider Your School's Demographics

When creating our leadership team for Response to Instruction, we considered our demographics. Yorktown Middle School is the sole middle school in the Yorktown Community School Corporation. Yorktown Community School Corporation currently serves 2,224 students and their families. Pleasant View Elementary is the primary school that feeds into Yorktown Elementary. Pleasant View contains kindergarten, first, and second grades. Yorktown Elementary School is an intermediate school building that houses third, fourth, and fifth grades. All of the students at Yorktown Elementary feed into one middle school, Yorktown

Middle School, and one high school, Yorktown High School. All of the Yorktown Community Schools are located on a campus area bordered by State Road 32, Tiger Drive, and County Road 50 South in Yorktown, Indiana.

Currently, Yorktown Middle School houses and educates 572 students. The student population includes a diversity of 93% Caucasian, 2% Asian, 2% African American, 2% Multiracial, and 1% Hispanic. The girl to boy ratio is approximately 1:1. Currently, there are 279 male students and 293 female students.

Approximately 60 students at Yorktown Middle School receive special education support services. Special education students are serviced under the Delaware-Blackford County Special Education Cooperative. The cooperative also provides contracted occupational and physical therapy to those students who qualify. Currently, of the 572 students enrolled at YMS, approximately 16% of the student body receives free lunch support and 10% receive reduced lunch benefits.

Yorktown Middle School annually participates in the State of Indiana's assessment ISTEP+. Yorktown Middle School regularly performs well as a building on these yearly assessments. The percentage of students at Yorktown Middle School passing both the Language Arts and Math sections (in the spring of 2009) was 77.7%, while the state average passing percentage was 71.4%.

How to Build Your Leadership Team

As mentioned many times throughout this book, this process CANNOT be done without all members of your school playing an active role in the process. However, you obviously cannot have the entire staff involved in every detail of the development

CHAPTER THREE

and implementation of a tiered instructional program. Eventually, it becomes essential to build a strong core team who will be the "cabinet" of your tiered instructional program. Choose team members who are able to provide expertise in specified areas of need for your building.

As an administrator, I focus a great deal on common sense and building relationships to define my style of leadership. However, just as any lifelong learner should do, I study successful people and read their leadership material. When thinking about how to set up this team and who I would invite to be a part of the team, I drew from two leaders: Coach John Wooden and John C. Maxwell. I took ideologies from their philosophies and blended them with my own to sort through the items I felt were essential for this team. I knew this team would be crucial to the very existence of the program. This team had to define RtI as a sustaining program and not the next trend or buzzword in education. We needed a team where all parties felt ownership in the program and were actively involved in the process, as opposed to a "top down" initiative. Implementing an initiative such as RtI requires a great deal of buy-in from the staff. By creating a team of teacher colleagues, the free flow of communication, information, and ideas was established, which fostered even more excitement within the faculty involved in the implementation.

So the time came for me to establish the core RtI team for Yorktown Middle School. As mentioned earlier, I drew upon two leaders and their philosophies, which I felt meshed with my leadership style. Using these guidelines, I began seeking those teacher leaders based on these ideals. "Shared thinking" is a trait that John C. Maxwell discussed in his book, *How Successful People Think*. As I reflected on the members of our staff, I continued to think back about a specific bulleted section of this book that focused on, "Getting the Right People Around the Table" (Maxwell, 2009). Among many items, Maxwell listed the following criteria for choosing members of a brainstorming team (Maxwell, 2009).

- People whose greatest desire is the success of the ideas.
- People who appreciate the strengths of others in areas where they are weak.
- People who place what is best for the team before their own desires.
- People who possess the maturity, experience, and success in the issue under discussion.
- People who will take ownership and responsibility for decisions.
- People who will leave the table with a "we" attitude and not a "me" attitude.

I certainly used many of these guidelines as a "litmus test" as I searched for the right combination of staff members.

Coach John Wooden is also a leader who has always captured my imagination with regards to his leadership style. In his book, *Wooden on Leadership*, he states,

> "I believe that you must have people around you willing to ask questions and express opinions, people who seek improvement for the organization rather than merely gaining favor with the boss. Look for these people when hiring and making promotion decisions. Remember: Failure is not fatal, but failure to change might be" (Wooden, 2005).

CHAPTER THREE

Using this perspective, I sought teachers who I knew would give me appropriate feedback, recommendations, and maximum devotion to the program.

The final piece of leadership philosophy that I drew upon while building the team was once again based on the work of John C. Maxwell, in his book, *Developing the Leaders Around You*. Maxwell writes:

"Am I effective in the areas I need to equip? This is a tough question that requires an honest answer. If the answer is 'no', the leader must locate a person, inside or outside the organization, effective in those areas who can do some of the training. Either that, or he had better go out and get himself equipped" (Maxwell, 1995).

There were certainly many areas identified in our RtI process where I was not equipped to be the administrative "expert." This was ultimately a crucial piece in many of the decisions regarding teacher selection for the core RtI leadership team. I needed a team of specialists.

Combining all of these philosophies as the backbone for my selection process, I identified the following members for our RtI team: two Special Education teachers, the school counselor, the school psychologist, the Language Arts classroom teacher, and myself.

The Special Education teachers were a natural choice for many reasons. First, their background knowledge and "toolbox" of different instructional approaches and programs made them teacher leaders throughout this initiative. Also, with the ramifications of RtI regarding identification for special education services, it was essential for these teachers to have a working knowledge and background of any student who worked through all of our tiers without success, who would be recommended for an educational evaluation.

Our school counselor was another member chosen for multiple reasons. The counselor will play a key role in any RtI program, in my opinion, due to their knowledge of student academic performance. In addition to this background knowledge on students, our counselor handles student class schedules and, within our program, I was certain there were going to be many students moving in and out of classes during our intervention times. Therefore, the expertise she brought to the table in these areas made her a mandatory piece of the puzzle.

The school psychologist was asked to participate and bring her expertise in analyzing large amounts of data and seeking out current research to share and analyze with the group. Another factor that makes it important for the school psychologist to be a part of the program is that he or she will eventually be one of the people conducting evaluations on any student recommended for special education, after the tier work has been identified as unsuccessful.

The final member was invited because of her ability to equip others in areas where I knew I did not have the appropriate expertise. Yorktown Middle School had a Language Arts teacher who recently received her Reading Specialist degree and had extensive knowledge on using Lexiles, ZPD, and multi-leveled curriculum. With our target on reading comprehension, it was once again an extremely easy decision to ask her to participate as a team member of the RtI process.

In addition to all of these educators being chosen for specific expertise, they all fit many of the other criteria that I established for members of the team. All members felt comfortable leading, speaking, and sharing their ideas rather than waiting for top-down directives. All of these women certainly thought of our students before any self-serving motives. They were self-driven and a hundred percent committed to making this program succeed. Thus, our team was born!

Quick Chapter Review

This chapter explains the following:
- How to consider your school's demographics
- How to build your leadership team

RECOLLECTIONS & REFLECTIONS
Chapter 3: The Leadership Team

1. After you finish the chapter, close the book and write down 3 words or phrases that immediately come to mind.

2. Write down two helpful pieces of information you learned.

3. Write down one question that you still have.

4. Write down one way that this chapter has changed your thinking about RtI.

5. Write down any ideas you have for how you might implement something from this chapter.

CHAPTER THREE

6. Write down a significant "ah-ha" moment you experienced while reading this chapter (if any).

7. Describe something from your professional experience that came to mind as you worked with the ideas in this chapter.

8. Write down any resources from the chapter, your discussions, or personal web surfing that would help in implementing RtI in your school.

9. Is the goal that you identified at the beginning of this experience still the same? If not, explain why it changed and then write down your new goal.

CHAPTER FOUR
PROFESSIONAL DEVELOPMENT

Jan Brown
Special Education Teacher & Behavioral Consultant

Heath Dudley
Principal

"In Interventions and Extensions class, we do an activity called Brain Gym. Because of Brain Gym, I have learned to focus." – Seventh Grade Girl

Schools must now respond to a national call for a multi-tiered system of instruction. Therefore, there exists a plethora of information on assessing needs in schools, intervening, monitoring responses, and preventing failure. There is not, however, a plethora information on how to prepare and continue to equip teachers and staff for the multi-tiered systems.

YMS wrestled with how to present this change in systems to staff, while simultaneously trying to get the system ready for use. The core team often felt they were only a few steps ahead of the staff they were leading. A document from the National Association of State Directors of Special Education, which is a blueprint for implementation, gives step-by-step directions for providing the framework for Indiana's Response to Instruction (Education NASP 2008). There are three components of the implementation protocol: 1) consensus building, 2) infrastructure building, and 3) implementation. In each component there are several actions and subsequent steps. For the first component alone, there are five actions and one to five steps for each action. "Wisdom from the field" suggested that consensus building alone could take several years. YMS was in a position in which we couldn't wait; we had to proceed through the three stages in an abbreviated amount of time.

Consensus Building

We began to build consensus by introducing our staff to the concept and terminology of RtI through a PowerPoint slide show given during the first RtI staff meeting. A condensed version of the slide show (figures 4.1 and 4.2) is provided on pages 52-53.

This initial meeting took place a few months before the end of the school year. The PowerPoint was developed utilizing information from literature, presentations, and information from the Special Education director. The core team was candid with the staff, explaining that they were only a few steps ahead in this process, nothing was written in stone, and the core team would work towards a system that ultimately met the needs of YMS students. Fortunately, YMS staff have a flexible, "can do" attitude.

Building Infrastructure

Within a month of introducing the information to the staff, and shortly before the end of the school year, we commenced training on administering a school-wide universal screen. Only those teachers who would be involved in the administration of the fluency assessment underwent training during YMS collaborative planning time, which occurs each day from 7:30 a.m. to 8:10 a.m. We copied scoring booklets and disbursed to those involved by the core team, along with clipboards and timers. To ensure fidelity of assessment, we rehearsed oral and written directions for the staff. The school psychologist, who is a specialist in the area of test validity, attended discussions concerning administration. We also shared directions for setting up classrooms with teachers who would be involved in the process.

After deciding to use the eighth period to provide RtI services, the next challenge for our team was deciding how to handle the teaching assignments. We were running out of time for teacher input, as we only had four weeks left in the school year. The best solution for teacher buy-in is choice. If teachers were given a choice, rather than just being told what they were teaching, we hoped they would be more accepting of the process and of the change to their traditional eighth period class. Our RtI Team developed a teacher survey to gauge their preferences on the level they wanted to teach. In April of 2009, we utilized collaboration time to educate our teachers on the philosophy and implementation process of RtI. Our principal explained how our school was going to begin RtI services beginning the following fall. He explained that all teachers would be teaching an Interventions and Extensions (I&E) class during eighth period. Teachers were instructed to complete the survey according to their preferences, with the understanding that the core team would endeavor to honor their requests.

The Leadership Team met a few times throughout the summer to finalize details of implementing Interventions and Exten-

Introducing RtI to Staff

WHAT IS RESPONSE TO INSTRUCTION?

1. It is a multi-tiered approach to the early identification and support of students with academic and behavioral needs.
2. It is an alternate means of delivering interventions that can lead to identification for special/gifted education.
3. It is a system shift to access intervention for students who previously never qualify for special services.
4. It is similar to a triage system whereby all are assessed and those most in need get the most attention.

COMPONENTS OF RTI

1. High quality, scientifically based classroom instruction
2. Tiered instruction
3. Universal screening
4. Probes into progress
5. Parent involvement

WHAT ARE PROBES?

1. Probes are a form of progress monitoring as are curriculum based measurement (CBM) or running records
2. Probes are brief measures of assessment
3. Examples of probes/progress monitors include:
   STAR, AR, and DIBELS

WHAT IS TIERED INSTRUCTION?

```
         T3
      Intensive
     Intervention

        T2
      Targeted
    Intervention

         T1
   School Wide Instruction
      that all receive
```

1. Tier 1 + 30 additional minutes instruction
2. 1-3 students per group, daily

3. Tier 1 + 30 additional minutes instruction
4. 3-6 students per group, 3 times per week

5. Instruction received by everyone
6. Addresses learning needs for majority 80% or better

figures 4.1 & 4.2

sions classes. As we proceeded through the process of making teacher assignments, we realized our first priority was to determine student placement. The number of teachers at each tier was dependent on how many students were placed at each level. The team gathered data on all students and their reading comprehension levels, based on the MAZE test, which they took in May. We also examined students' ZPD levels, based on their latest STAR test. Once we grouped students, the next step was to determine how many teachers were needed for each tier. We tallied up the teacher surveys and suggested teaching assignments based upon the surveys.

Implementation

Upon returning to a new school year in the fall, the core team had the task of presenting a new universal screen to faculty, a new eighth period, which would house Interventions and Extensions (see figure 4.3), and new curricula for the Intervention period. Professional development sessions occurred during faculty meetings, collaboration times, and preparation periods of individual teachers. Two videos modeling how to hold a book conference and how to do Brain Gym exercises (Dennison, 1986) were made available for teachers. Because teachers had already experienced a universal screen with DIBELS, it was a fairly easy task to transition to the MAZE assessment for another universal screen. To equip teachers for the new Interventions and Extensions period, the core team had to have both short-range and long-range plans in place. The short-range plans included what the teachers would be doing from the first moment that they received students. When the core team initially presented the system change, they

Interventions	Extensions
• Leveled Readers • Book Conferencing • Toolbox - Test Prep • Purpose: To Remediate	• 1-2 Toolbox Activities / day • 20-25 Min of Reading • Book Conferencing • Purpose: To Accelerate

figure 4.3

promised the teachers that curriculum would be directed and provided for them and that they would not have the additional burden of prepping for yet another period. (The curriculum that had been purchased for use in Interventions and Extensions had not yet arrived and so an interim curriculum was warranted.) The long-range development included refining some of the initial plans and adding the newly purchased curriculums.

During the first two weeks of school, teachers were given a ten day plan, which included a scripted description of the class, discussion about the new class, getting acquainted activities, school handbook review, and organizational lessons. After the first two weeks, teachers were given a semi-permanent, daily lesson plan as a sample to meet our beginning of the year needs.

Part of the professional development was to train teachers on the use of Brain Gym, a trademarked program which incorporates movement to enhance whole brain learning. Teachers spent part of a professional development period trying the activities they would be teaching, such as Lazy Eights and the Cross Crawl (Dennison, 1986). This lighthearted comical time was much needed during the stressful time of starting a new year and a new system. It was great fun to see one's colleagues in unusual looking poses and movements designed to develop muscle memory. We even made a video for teachers modeling the correct movements for the eight different Brain Gym exercises, as well as making a small poster with the names of the eight exercises for each classroom.

The staff also studied the Eight Pillars of Executive Control (Cox, 2008). Teachers were given activities to foster executive functioning skills (EFS). These EFS activities would be a part of the daily lesson plans for the Interventions and Extensions period. These eight pillars are:

- Initiating Action – Getting Started
- Flexible Thinking – Shifting Focus and Pace
- Sustaining Attention – Duration and Intensity
- Organization – Managing Space
- Planning – Managing Time
- Working Memory – Retaining Information
- Self-Awareness – Gaining Self Knowledge
- Regulating Emotions – Under or Over Reacting

Activities were designed and given to staff to be used at the beginning of each Interventions and Extensions period; these activities generally addressed one of the eight pillars. For example, one lesson in the student handbook was on how to set up a daily plan. Students had several examples to choose and to use. That lesson fit into the Organization pillar. Also, we had students complete many interest inventories which fit under the Self-Awareness pillar. Each lesson was under one of the Eight Pillars of Executive Control.

CHAPTER FOUR

The lead team's attention towards professional development has now turned to strengthening the core curriculum. How are we teaching reading? Who is teaching reading? Does everyone know how to teach reading? Are we administering other assessments to be used in our "triangulation of data" with fidelity?

Quick Chapter Review

The path or stages that YMS has followed for professional development include:

- Consensus building with staff on definitions and concepts
- Building infrastructure
- Learning to administer a universal screen or progress monitor
- Surveying teachers for choices in their involvement
- Implementation
- Providing instructions on new curricula for intervention
- Supporting intervention teachers
- Examining the core curriculum; how can we make it more secure?

RECOLLECTIONS & REFLECTIONS
Chapter 4: Professional Development

1. After you finish the chapter, close the book and write down 3 words or phrases that immediately come to mind.

2. Write down two helpful pieces of information you learned.

3. Write down one question that you still have.

4. Write down one way that this chapter has changed your thinking about RtI.

5. Write down any ideas you have for how you might implement something from this chapter.

6. Write down a significant "ah-ha" moment you experienced while reading this chapter (if any).

7. Describe something from your professional experience that came to mind as you worked with the ideas in this chapter.

8. Write down any resources from the chapter, your discussions, or personal web surfing that would help in implementing RtI in your school.

9. Is the goal that you identified at the beginning of this experience still the same? If not, explain why it changed and then write down your new goal.

CHAPTER FIVE
ASSESSMENT

Jan Brown
Special Education Teacher & Behavioral Consultant

"Interventions and Extensions class has helped me improve my reading scores. My scores on the STAR reading test improved. I can understand what the author is trying to tell me, the reader. I have read more books this year than I have in a long time." – Eighth Grade Girl

Jim Wright from Syracuse City School District in New York writes that "the measurement of a child's school abilities is just as important as the teaching of those skills." Shores and Chester (2008) assert, "When decisions regarding assessment are made with the student in mind, the outcomes become more relevant to what we are striving to achieve in the classroom." In other words, an authentic system of assessment serves as a tool to measure learning and guide decision making.

Assessment is as old as public school, but assessment that will inform and guide efficiently has not always been available. When YMS began a review of the available literature on a multi-tiered system of instruction, or Response to Instruction (as Indiana named this system), it became clear that an alternative but efficient system of assessment was warranted. YMS had plenty of data, but that data came at the expense of instructional time, and one more assessment would not be tolerated.

Why Universal Screening?

Toward an alternative system of assessment, The Indiana Department of Education recommended that school-wide universal screening be conducted to reflect the effectiveness of the core curriculum and instruction to identify the students most in need of interventions or extensions. This universal screen would include a baseline and at least two additional screens during the year. The universal screen would answer the primary question of whether or not the instruction and curriculum were sufficient. If less than 80% of the screened population were successful, then the fidelity of instruction and the research base of the curriculum would need to be evaluated (IDOE, 2009). This percentage is also recommended by the National Association of Special Education Directors (Zillich, June Lucas, NASP, NEA, 2009). The second question, to be answered by the universal screen, would be who needs extensions and who needs interventions. These universal screens would be brief and easy to administer. Additionally, IDOE recommended that the screens must be of equivalent difficulty. Once a universal screen had been given, then progress monitoring assessments should be given over time to assess a student's response to instruction. This frequent progress monitoring, with additional brief assessments, would satisfy the need for alignment or linkage to instructional outcomes. Assessments must be used to inform curriculum decisions. Traditional assessments have limited samples of the critical skills needed and often give students different tasks than the ones actually needed (Hosp, Hosp, & Howell, 2007).

What Target Skill? Which Screen?

In our corporation, there was much debate about what to screen and what tool to use. YMS decided that there were three areas of need: 1) reading, 2) math, and 3) behavior. YMS decided to tackle one area at a time, so the first would be reading. The next decision was whether to assess reading fluency or reading comprehension. Hosp, Hosp and Howell (2007) state that Oral Reading Fluency (ORF) is a good predictor of future reading performance. The fluency company Read Naturally asserts that fluency is a strong predictor of how a student will score on high-stakes assessments designed to measure higher-order reading skills (Davidson & Towner, 2001). Hosp, Hosp, and Howell further defined a Maze test as an even better predictor of future reading performance for students in grades four or higher. The authors also stated that the Maze test appeared to have slightly better face validity than ORF for its relationship to comprehension.

The ORF is a decoding assessment, while the Maze is a comprehension assessment (see figure 5.1). The ORF consists of three grade-level passages, which are fiction, nonfiction, and representative of the general curriculum. The passages for grades six through eight are organized to ensure the same level of difficulty. The three passages are given one at a time and in one sitting. Students read orally, while an adult records errors and time. The mean, not the median score, of the number of words read correctly in one minute is calculated. A re-tell component can be given to offer additional information about reading comprehension.

The Maze test consists of one graded passage with words omitted. Three choices are given for each word omitted. One is correct, and two are incorrect. Students read the passage silently and choose a word to circle each time they come to three choices. Students are given three minutes to read the passage and circle choices. Both assessments are brief, but while ORF is administered individually, the Maze test can be administered to a group.

Oral Reading Fluency (ORF)

Teachers	Students
• Listen to individual student • Time • Record errors during assessment • Solicit a timed oral re-tell • Record number of words spoken	• Read orally for one minute • Retell passage in own words for one minute

Maze Comprehension

Teachers	Students
• Monitor group for effort and direction adherence • Score errors and total number of words read	• Read a passage silently for three minutes • Circle correct word to complete 1-2 blank parts of every sentence

figure 5.1

CHAPTER FIVE

To begin our first phase of implementing a multi-tiered system, we began with an ORF in late spring as a universal screen to target students for the following year. Alas, the simple and only reason we chose the ORF was because we already had it on hand. While we preferred the Maze assessment for our age group, it was not available, so we chose the DIBELS assessment (one form of ORF). Once the assessment was administered, we were faced with the reality of graphing the results by hand, finding the time to assess the whole building, and copying the DIBELS fluency booklets for all. It is important to note that while we made a decision to go with a Maze test, we found the fluency assessment a good process to walk through as a school. We gained valuable information about administering a school-wide screen. For example, we learned that it took five to six adults per class to administer a fluency assessment in one period. Also, teachers discovered that while they had many students who read fluently, many of those same students did poorly when given the retell portion of the fluency assessment.

LOCAL VS. COMMERCIAL ASSESSMENT

The gold standard for assessment began in Special Education in the late '70s. It involved making brief assessments directly from the current curriculum. My Special Education degree in the '80s involved a course which taught one how to make an assessment using local curriculum. Initially and ideally we thought we would make our own Maze tests so that the assessment could come directly from the curriculum, but to generate such an assessment for Special Education students alone is quite different from creating an assessment to be used with the entire school population.

According to Hosp, Hosp, and Howell (2007), we would need to generate passages that included at least 300 words and 42 deleted words with three replacement words each. Shores and Chester (2008) state that passages should be around 400 words with every seventh word replaced with three choices. Those three choices would be the correct choice and two incorrect words with similar numbers of letters. One of the replacements would need to be a near distracter while the other incorrect choice would need to be a far distracter. We would need three passages for the universal screening and then around thirty more for progress monitoring. All passages would need to be the same difficulty level. Also, when textbook adoption years rolled around, new protocols would need to be developed. This task seemed daunting. Additionally, we would not have any national norms to compare our results.

Therefore, YMS decided that a commercially-bought Maze assessment would still satisfy curriculum alignment, by targeting a specific skill being taught, and, as a bonus, we would have national norms, in addition to local norms, when we analyzed the data. So I spent the summer searching for commercially prepared Maze tests. Two sources were available: 1) Yearly Progress Pro, CTB/McGraw-Hill, and 2) AIMSweb, Pearson. The products were similar, but the Yearly Progress Pro was more expensive. In the midst of a recession and budget cuts, I recommended that we purchase the AIMSweb Maze reading assessment. Our administration happily approved! And thankfully, this product would give us not only pre-made passages to use for benchmarks and progress monitoring, but also graphs of our data to create an aimline or progress toward a benchmark (see Appendix B). For example, one student was able to visually see that he had four data

CHAPTER FIVE

points above his aimline. He was also able to see that his trend line was increasing.

What About the Data we Already Have?

In the meantime, the data from the universal screen, the ORF, was used to start the new school year. Armed with a system borrowed from another school, the data was ranked along with ISTEP scores and Orchard skills assessment. Points were assigned to each assessment (see figure 5.2). The points assigned to the state-

How Our Scores Were Ranked

ISTEP

(1) DNP
(2) Pass
(3) Pass Plus

ORCHARD

(1) 0-23%
(2) 26%-75%
(3) 76-100%

FLUENCEY/DIBELS

(1) Intensive
(2) Strategic
(3) Benchmark

figure 5.2

wide testing were assigned according to the descriptions given by the state, while the Orchard points were assigned according to average percentages of the class in which the student took the assessment. The DIBELS points were assigned according to the descriptions generated by DIBELS.

Using this system, if you accumulated six to nine points, you were placed in Tier 1. If you had four or five points, you were placed into Tier 2. If you had three or less points, you were placed in Tier 3. As an example, Student A could pass ISTEP earning two points, get a 28% on Orchard earning two more points, and be ranked by the DIBELS classification system earning one point. This would give Student A five points. This student then would be placed into Tier 2 for intervention. Along the way, it was determined that we had no real defense for how this ranking system was formed, specifically how points were assigned. The Minnesota Department of Education recommends that a triangulation of data be used to analyze needs—using one screening assessment to provide a preliminary student placement and using other data to gather multiple perspectives on those already identified by the universal screen as below benchmark. The ranking system we used (ISTEP, Orchard, and DIBELS) qualified three pieces of data considered to be equal. YMS decided that in the future, when the Maze test was used as a universal screening tool, we would discard the ranking system and simply prioritize students in need, based on the benchmarks provided by national norms. Furthermore, we would utilize Indiana state testing scores (ISTEP) and reading Zones of Proximal Development as supplemental information to guide informed decisions. We also decided to record our decision-making process to track our rationale for placing individual students into tiers.

CHAPTER FIVE

How Do we Place Students?

The first universal screen, ORF, targeted oral reading fluency and had been given at the end of the school year. Students were placed in either Interventions or Extensions classes based on the data from the ranking system. In the fall of the next year, a second universal screen was implemented with the Maze, in place of the ORF. Armed with this new data, the school counselor, the reading teacher and specialist, and a Special Education representative sat down to analyze the data. Students who were at the tenth percentile were considered well below average and immediately flagged for intervention. Also, students were flagged between the tenth and twenty-fifth percentile and considered to be below average. Students who were above the twenty-fifth percentile were considered average, above average, or well above average. These students were placed in Extensions classes designed to extend their reading abilities. Those who were well above average were considered for Advanced Placement classes.

Once this initial flagging was complete, the data team further red-flagged students whose Maze scores did not align with ISTEP and STAR scores. Twenty-six seventh and eighth graders were considered for review out of approximately 402 students. There were several types of anomalies that accounted for this group. Some students received an average score on the universal screen but did not pass the Language Arts portion of ISTEP and scored several grade levels below on the STAR reading assessment. Another group did not do well on the universal screen or the STAR but did pass the ISTEP. All of the students flagged had Zone of Proximal Development (ZPDs) on the STAR reading test that were one to four years below grade level. These students were carefully discussed to determine why their scores were not consistent and to determine their placement. In the end, all but three students were flagged to be progress monitored so that time would show decision-making patterns. We made some interesting discoveries about these students: 1) Some were English as a Second Language (ESL) students, 2) Some were identified as Special Education students and had other issues clouding their assessment results, and 3) Other students were borderline in one subject area. The data team further discussed the probability that some students did not take one or more tests seriously. We discovered that a student could fail ISTEP Language Arts but still adequately comprehend reading. ISTEP assesses more than just reading comprehension. (To view an example of the data we utilized for decision rules, see Appendices C and D.) The universal screen (Maze) was the primary source of data with ISTEP and STAR ZPD as secondary pieces of data.

What the Maze Told us About our School

Our initial universal screen, using the oral reading fluency, revealed that 76% of our seventh graders and 74% of our eighth graders met benchmark. YMS kept in mind that "the false positive rate of early screening may be as high as 50%" (Dickman, 2006). This information meant that as many as half of the students we identified as "at risk" might not be at risk. Our second universal screen, using the Maze comprehension assessment, revealed that 80% of our seventh graders and 77% of our eighth graders met benchmark. Armed with numbers that are probably closer to skill levels, YMS believed that these results were close enough to warrant an in-depth look at our first goal of a multi-tiered system, which was to scrutinize the core curriculum. Is the core curriculum secure and being taught with fidelity? Are we implementing scientifically-based reading instruction in the core curriculum? Is it careful, faithful, and systematic? Are we differentiating instruction and monitoring progress in the core curriculum? Do staff members understand that fidelity does not mean teaching every activity or asking every question on every page of a teacher's edition? Do staff members understand that if you don't teach every activity or ask every question, that you also don't randomly choose activities or questions without paying attention to student needs in your classroom? Do teachers understand fidelity does not mean incorporating favorite stories, strategies, and activities without regard to student need (Jay, 2009)?

When Do we Progress Monitor?

Meanwhile, Interventions and Extensions classes were set up, and it was time to turn our attention to progress monitoring. Many sources were considered as to how often we would progress monitor. Hosp, Hosp, and Howell (2007) recommend progress monitoring once or even twice per week. Shores and Chester (2008) recommend evaluation on a regular basis: weekly, biweekly or even monthly, depending on individual student need. The Minnesota Department of Education recommends progress monitoring every two to three weeks. Dr. Rebecca Martinez Reid (2009), Indiana University, recommends every week, but no less than every month. Yuri, Schleich, and Spradlin (2009) assert that "performance samples be collected once per week to three times a year depending on the intensity of intervention."

YMS chose to progress monitor every two weeks. The students who were already identified as eligible for special education would receive a more intensive curriculum and would be progress monitored weekly. An important philosophy that YMS adopted was that no students would be considered Tier 3 unless they already had an IEP or until they were progress monitored and determined not to be responding to the core curriculum and/or their intervention time. In other words, we did not simply plunk students into a third tier of intervention without data to support our decision.

How Often Do we Look at Data? How Many Points Do we Need?

At what interval should we analyze the biweekly data collected during progress monitoring? It was clear that the number of weeks and the number of points were both important. One recommendation for academic skills analysis was a period of eight to ten weeks or one grading period to evaluate any Response to Instruction (Rathvon, 2008). Aimsweb and June Lucas Zillich (2009), from the National Association of School Psychologists, recommend evaluating data after three points, which could be three weeks or five weeks depending on how often one is progress monitoring. MacArthur Elementary School evaluates after six data points, which could be six to twelve weeks. Hosp, Hosp, and Howell (2007) recommend six to eight data points. Ron Benner (2008) recommends a minimum of three weeks and at least six points.

A common thread, emphasized in all the recommendations, was the importance of looking for patterns in the data, regardless of the weekly intervals or data points. YMS needed to decide over how many weeks the data should be collected and how many data points were needed to prompt a review. YMS is currently looking toward a decision rule of four data points over eight weeks for most students and eight data points over eight weeks for those getting more intensive interventions.

How Do we Identify Patterns to Inform Intervention?

It is important to note that literature uses the word "goal line" and "aimline" interchangeably. YMS defines the line made by a baseline score and the desired end score as the aimline. Furthermore, the goal is the desired end score. The Curriculum Based Assessment by Jim Wright (2009) uses these rules:

- If three successive data points lie above the aimline, instructor adjusts aimline upward.
- If three successive data points lie below the aimline, the instructor changes instruction.
- If three successive data points lay around the aimline, continue with instruction.

Ron Benner (2008) uses these guidelines:

- If four points are above the goal line, then increase the goal.
- If four points are below the goal line, then change teaching.
- If four points are both above and below the goal line, then keep collecting data until the four-point rule can be used.

Another presenter (source unknown) at the Indiana conference on Response to Instruction (2009) handed out rules for visual analysis of data. Those rules, based on the four most recent consecutive data points were:

- If four data points are all above the goal line, keep the current intervention and increase the goal.
- If four data points are all below the goal line, keep the current goal and modify the intervention.
- If four data points are neither above nor below the goal line, maintain the current goal, maintain intervention, continue data collection, and review data.

These slightly different models all look for patterns above and/or below the aimline. YMS decided to: 1) Increase the goal (end score) for patterns above the aimline, regardless of skill level, 2) Keep current goals and change instruction for those with patterns below the aimline, and 3) Continue data collection for all.

How Do Students Move Within the System?

Bi-weekly data was evaluated once students had accumulated four data points, over a period of eight weeks (one week short of a grading period), in addition to the baseline, which was the universal screen at year's start. Progress monitoring did not start immediately following the universal screen for the very simple reason that the core team needed to take a deep breath and slow down. We were trying to do too much too quickly, and we needed to make sure we were moving ahead wisely. And so, the four data points occurred at about the same time as the second universal screen. After the second universal screen, we were able to look at data from all classes and adjust Interventions and Extensions

CHAPTER FIVE

classes. It was an important time to make changes and basically give a shake up to all classes. Middle school students quickly ascertain the level of the class they are in, and so movement signaled progress to them. They knew they were working towards four data points above their aimline. This mass movement signaled a tone that the effort you put into the assessments and interventions did have results.

Two Case Studies

I will never forget the look on one student's face when her scores increased. She had been placed in an Interventions class with the lowest assessment scores. Her first universal screen was 21 correct, which was right on the bubble for meeting benchmark. Her ISTEP Language Arts score was sixty-six points below proficiency and her STAR reading score was four to five grade levels below her current grade. As she participated in the Interventions class and was progress monitored, her correct responses scores were as follows: 20, 37, 27, 33, 28. Her second universal screen was 33 correct. Her face on the day she scored 37 was like the sun breaking through a storm cloud. Her face was pure satisfaction and joy. Imagine the pure joy and satisfaction that I, too, experienced at that moment as her teacher.

Consider another student who also had some of the lowest assessment scores on the universal screen. This student, who had been placed in an Interventions class, created a petition that he circulated amongst his peers. The petition was to eliminate eighth period Interventions and Extensions classes and make eighth period a study hall. This student was, at the time, loud and verbose in Interventions class. He presented himself as a student who was defensive and in need of attention. As he participated reluctantly in direct instruction for decoding skills and was progress monitored, a gradual change came over him. He became more respectful towards the teacher and peers in the class. He began to take the lessons more seriously, and he became more serious as a student. His correct responses scores were: 13, 11, 7, and 10 after an initial baseline of 6 correct responses on a universal screen. While other students had moved on to other Interventions classes due to their progress, this student had not. He knew his scores well and said, "I will do whatever it takes to get a score to move on and out of this class. Please Mrs. Brown, whatever it takes." This student currently takes his Interventions class seriously, puts forth good effort, and is a delightful student to work with. He is a far cry from the petition-signing days. His scores are not at benchmark, but he is no longer avoiding his reading deficits.

How Do we Maintain Fidelity in Assessment?

The first universal screen, ORF, was given the third week of school. The second universal screen, the Maze, was administered the first week of second semester. The third universal screen will be given in early- to mid-May a few weeks before school is dismissed for summer break. All universal screens are given eighth period, which is the last period of the day in which all students are enrolled in the Interventions and Extensions classes. Progress monitoring also takes place eighth period every week or every other week depending on intensity of intervention. One staff member downloads the cover sheets, the Maze, scripted directions, and answer keys each time the assessment is given. Teachers are then responsible for making copies for their classes.

CHAPTER FIVE

In order to promote fidelity of the assessment, the assessments all happen at the start of class, and the office staff is alerted not to make any announcements. Teachers utilize a script as well as timers that are displayed on projection screens or Smart Boards. If a teacher has a substitute on the day of the assessment, then an experienced staff person usually administers the assessment for the substitute teacher. Teachers then score the assessments and submit scores within 24 hours. Scores are entered by the lead data team. Typically, progress reports are available for teachers to access and print for students the next day during their Interventions or Extensions time. Absent students are assessed as soon as they return to school. Results of universal screens are placed in a common teacher area so that teachers can see percentages of improvement for each grade level. Detailed reports are given to teams and class reports are available via assessment software for Interventions and Extensions teachers.

What we Have Learned About Assessment?

- It is easy to administer a universal screen and progress monitoring assessments.
- It is a lot of work to manage the assessment data software.
- It is a lot of work to make big schedule changes at one time.
- Students are motivated by objective reports that represent one skill.
- Students take the assessments seriously if they believe true change will happen.
- Teachers bond with classes and have a hard time when

students move in and out of classes due to progress.
- Students get excited seeing their scores increase.
- Students are very quiet during assessments.
- Assessment scores generated by AIMsweb are easy for parents to understood.

Reflections

After countless debates, disagreements and discussions, the authors have discovered a few truths about assessment. These truths are as follows:

- Assessments must be chosen to match the skills areas of concern.
- Assessments must have screening or benchmark and progress monitoring capabilities.
- Screening and monitoring must be brief and easy to administer.
- Decision rules must be determined to dictate student placement in the appropriate class (this is the hardest).
- Most importantly, the lead team has discovered that we must never stop evaluating what is and what is not working.

Quick Chapter Review

This chapter discusses the following questions concerning universal screening:

- What target skill? Which screen?
- Local or commercial assessment?
- What about data you already have?

- How do we place students?
- What did the Maze tell us about our school?
- When do we progress monitor?
- How often do we look at the data? How many points are needed?
- How do we identify patterns to inform intervention?
- How do students move within the system?
- How do we maintain fidelity in assessment?
- What have we learned about assessment?

RECOLLECTIONS & REFLECTIONS
Chapter 5: Assessment

1. After you finish the chapter, close the book and write down 3 words or phrases that immediately come to mind.

2. Write down two helpful pieces of information you learned.

3. Write down one question that you still have.

4. Write down one way that this chapter has changed your thinking about RtI.

5. Write down any ideas you have for how you might implement something from this chapter.

6. Write down a significant "ah-ha" moment you experienced while reading this chapter (if any).

7. Describe something from your professional experience that came to mind as you worked with the ideas in this chapter.

8. Write down any resources from the chapter, your discussions, or personal web surfing that would help in implementing RtI in your school.

9. Is the goal that you identified at the beginning of this experience still the same? If not, explain why it changed and then write down your new goal.

CHAPTER SIX
RTI FROM A TEACHER'S PERSPECTIVE

Amy Carney-Heath
Reading Specialist & Teacher

"Interventions and Extensions class has helped my reading score go up. It helps me actually get into books, and now I enjoy books. My AR score is higher than ever right now. I have passed 24 out of 26 AR tests this year and that's awesome for me. Last year, it wasn't good. I didn't even pass ISTEP."

– Seventh Grade Student

Learning About RtI

"Response to [Instruction] as a model for boosting student achievement has taken off like wildfire. When it comes to research on how best to implement the process for students in middle and high school, though, the flame abruptly fizzles out. There's little research that is specific to secondary schools…" (Samuels, 2009).

During the year 2008, I learned that RtI was the nation's answer to individualized instruction for every student. Articles began to appear in education magazines and journals, and the International Reading Association claimed: "RtI is to focus on providing more effective instruction by encouraging earlier intervention for students experiencing difficultly learning to read" (IDEA, 2004). Even though I didn't really understand RtI, I agreed with the philosophy that every student needed individualized instruction, especially reading instruction; however, I could not imagine what individualized instruction would look like for each student in an entire school building.

After our leadership team conducted a review of the literature, we soon discovered that no one really knew what RtI looked like at the middle school or high school levels. In fact, when we attended a large RtI conference, the leader discovered that I was a reading specialist in middle school and asked me to speak about RtI! I was just sitting in the audience, when I quickly realized that RtI was an abbreviation on paper which many educators did not fully understand.

RtI is simply tiered instruction; to me, tiered instruction was an old term applied to a new abbreviation. If you're a reading specialist, you immediately think about ability or flexible reading groups. If you're licensed in gifted education, you think about grouping your highest achievers together and offering them enrichment opportunities. Master teachers in regular classrooms already supplement the curriculum to meet individual student's needs. Therefore, RtI is not really a new idea; it just offers differentiated instruction to all students in an entire building.

The purpose of RtI is to teach all students, high ability learners and struggling learners, so that no one misses an opportunity for instruction. It is individualized instruction in mass quantity.

Working to Implement RtI

In order to implement this philosophy school wide, the principal, counselor, and all teachers must work together. Fortunately, in my school building, our teachers share a passionate love of learning and are willing to try any instructional method if it means that student achievement will improve.

RtI provided a new avenue for our teachers to come together 1) to review students' needs and 2) to establish building-wide goals and parameters that would foster successful reading for all students. We needed to assess each student and then design curriculum to match that assessment. If the core curriculum is not effective, then the teacher must have an alternative curriculum available. Interventions would offer a supplemental curriculum for struggling learners who did not meet grade-level expectations. Extensions would offer enrichment for students who were meeting or exceeding grade-level benchmarks. Implementing RtI school wide would now provide all teachers with the necessary curriculum options to match the assessments of each and every student.

Using Assessments to Make Decisions About Student Placement in Interventions or Extensions

In the beginning, we administered a universal screener, the MAZE test, to determine the needs of all students. Our Special Education teacher worked diligently with our school psychologist to conduct the assessment school wide. We used the universal screener as our primary means of making initial tier decisions.

Our students also took a STAR reading test, which provided a ZPD (Zone of Proximal Development) range. We used the ZPD range to provide a skeleton of the students' learning abilities. If the student's score was low, the student's range was narrow.

If the student's score was high, the student's range was broad. As educators and a reading specialist, we knew the ZPD range was not perfect. We had studied Instructional Reading Levels (IRL), Lexile levels, and other readability formulas. We appreciated the concepts behind the Northwest Evaluation Assessment but realized that we did not have the funds required to administer the test. We knew if we used the ZPD range, the assessment matched our leveled Accelerated Reader resources, and we needed to use what we already had for the benefit of the teachers and the students. The ZPD scores and state testing data was especially helpful to Interventions teachers as they planned instruction.

Creating Research Based Instruction

As the RtI team wrestled with student placement, we also wrestled with finding appropriate curriculum materials to meet students' needs as identified by the assessments. The Special Education teacher and I had the responsibility of creating curriculum, with the input of teachers and local university professors. In a short time frame, our team needed to identify Tier 2 reading materials. For Tier 3, we had already chosen a multi-sensory reading program.

Before I recommended a reading curriculum to our team, I reviewed the research on effective reading instructional strategies. I also reviewed my notes from various workshops and training seminars. My teaching career has been influenced by my philosophy of reading instruction. Influences included Marie Clay, Pat Cunningham, Dottie Hall, Irene Fountas, Gay Su Pinnell, Sam Miller, and Francine Johnston. I considered the strengths of Clay's Reading Recovery program (1993), Cunningham's Four

Blocks program (2006), and Bear, Templeton, and Johnston's Making Words program. (2007) All of these programs considered developmentally-appropriate individual instruction for each student. Even though these programs were created for lower and upper elementary classrooms, I knew that the principles of the programs could extend to middle and high school curricula. In all of these programs, I liked the fact that the assessment and curriculum worked together to create meaningful learning experiences for individual students. I reviewed many programs, but I knew I was looking for a program that offered leveled texts with leveled assessments and a focus on individual instruction. I also knew that the program had to be middle-school friendly. If students were struggling, they did not need a "baby" text to remind them. Students needed to have opportunities to build their confidence with developmentally appropriate text, text that targeted instruction and met their needs. Whether the need was a second grade reader for an eighth grader or a first grade reader for a seventh grader, the need had to be met. The student had to be served. The integrity of the student had to be honored.

In the 1990s, I went to a Reading Recovery Conference in North Carolina where Marie Clay gave a lecture to teachers. I never forgot that experience. It was a great privilege to hear Clay speak on meeting the needs of struggling readers. During her talks, Clay conveyed that if a student says they do not like to read, it is often because they are a struggling reader. Once the student learns to read, they usually like to read. Clay inspired and encouraged me to believe that the struggling reader could learn to read with effective interventions and it was my job to equip teachers with those strategies that work, such as running records and miscue analysis (Clay, 2000).

While Clay focused on elementary age students, I could see how her principles also applied to middle school and high school students. Clay wrote, "A text is at a students' independent reading level if they can read it with about 95% accuracy" (Clay, 1993). When I thought about Clay's insight into students' independent reading levels, I was determined to find a curriculum that supported Clay's philosophy. In addition, I wanted our students to have an easy way to find a "just right" book when they went to the library. At this point, I thought of Fountas and Pinnell's words, "We need to be sure we're matching the right books with the right students" (2008). When I heard Clay's philosophy mixed with Fountas and Pinnell's voices, I knew our students needed just-right texts at their independent reading levels.

Providing Leveled Readers

Making the just-right books available for each of our students became a priority. We decided to order level E, F, and G readers from McGraw-Hill's SRA curriculum (2008). These readers would allow us to remediate through acceleration and offer curriculum for students performing at grade levels 4 through 8. After we tested the students, we realized that we should have ordered books at lower levels, too, because our students also needed grades 1 to 3 leveled readers.

My principal and I worked with our librarian to level our middle school library (see figure 6.1). While this leveling system is common in an elementary school library, it is uncommon in middle school and high school. We believed that all students should be able to choose what they wanted to read. Having leveled texts in our library suddenly gave both our Interventions and

CHAPTER SIX

figure 6.1. Red dots placed on the lower spine of the book are used to indicate that the book is a leveled book. The student opens the books to discover the book level.

Extensions students more book choices. This in itself fostered a sense of competence and confidence for many of our struggling readers.

Teaching Teachers to Teach Students how to Find Academically-Appropriate Books

For the first three months of school, I worked with every teacher and every class. I modeled the process of finding a book at a student's independent reading level. I made a chart to inform teachers and students (see figure 6.2). I organized all of the ZPD levels by ability, and we asked other support staff to pull books to make the process teacher-friendly.

Because we asked Science, Social studies, and Algebra teachers to teach an Interventions or Extensions class, we wanted all teachers to be knowledgeable about student book choice.

How to Check a Book Out at Your Independent Reading Level

Your Reading Teacher will give you a copy of your STAR Reading Diagnostic Report.

1. Find your ZPD range on your report.
2. Choose an AR Book in your ZPD range.
3. Read the title and summary.
4. Choose one page to read in the book.

   a. If the book is **just right** for you, you can pronounce and understand ALL but one or two words, and you can retell most of what you read.

   b. If the book is too **difficult**, you cannot pronounce or do not know the meaning of five words on the page, and you cannot retell what you read.

   c. If the book is too **easy**, you can read and pronounce and understand all of the words and retell everything you have read. If this is the case, choose a different book in your ZPD Range.

---

figure 6.2. We provided this handout for each teacher to post in their classroom.

Upon the research findings of Clay, Cunningham, Fountas, and Pinnell, I created an outline for a bulletin board to help all teachers find just-right books for their students at a student's Zone of Proximal Development.

CHAPTER SIX

Encouraging Students to Go to the Library

Our principal used helpful graphs (see figure 6.3 below) to track student library usage, and then sent the information to teachers. The principal sent tallied book check-out graphs via e-mail to all teachers. Seeing these results in graph form encouraged teachers to promote the library, as they saw students checking out more and more books. The graphs proved to teachers that their efforts

Figure 6.3: Yorktown Middle School Library Circulation - Monthly Comparison

Month	2008 - 2009	2009 - 2010
Aug	444	1171
Sept	1607	2147
Oct	1346	2736
Nov	1604	2770
Dec	762	1282

made a difference. When I first saw our principal's graph, I was shocked by how our teachers' efforts really changed students' library habits.

TRAINING AND MODELING FOR INTERVENTIONS CLASSES

Once classroom teachers equipped and empowered students to find books at their independent reading levels, I started visiting the classrooms of Interventions teachers only. Later in the year, our new SRA curriculum had arrived, and I was anxious for implementation. We organized the leveled readers (books) by grade level. I decided to put the readers in individual folders for easy teacher access. I labeled the folders in accordance with the curriculum guide (see figure 6.4). In addition, I modeled a week's worth of lessons for the individual teachers.

I also demonstrated how teachers could use varied strategies such as silent reading, partner reading, or guided reading. We

figure 6.4. We have five crates of SRA books from McGraw-Hill. The books are organized by grade level.

CHAPTER SIX

made reading journals for each student, which allowed students to practice their comprehension strategies. We modeled strategies that could be used before reading, during reading, and after reading (see Appendix E). These preparations were made to help all teachers feel empowered to teach reading strategies which they could in turn utilize across the curriculum.

I also modeled vocabulary lessons, including the guess and check strategy (see Appendix F). Teachers would give a word list to students based on the lesson in the leveled reader. Students would guess the definition of the words. After students had time to guess, teachers told students the answers and gave students the opportunities to correct their answers. Because the McGraw Leveled Reader program has a controlled vocabulary component, students reviewed words frequently. Students studied not only how a word looked phonetically, but also the meaning of the word.

Later, teachers integrated semantic mind maps to increase the rate of words learned. The International Reading Association published an article titled, "Classifying and Super Word Web: Two Strategies to Improve Productive Vocabulary," by Andrew Johnson and Jay Rasmussen (1998). This article led to semantic mind maps and an outstanding website with templates, located at http://t4.jordan.k12.ut.us/teacher_resources/inspiration_templates/. This site allowed teachers to load semantic mind maps on their computers and generate them through their in-focus projector. Quickly, teachers could begin a vocabulary lesson with the prescribed words from the leveled curriculum.

From this process, teachers learned that struggling readers needed support. Teachers noted that students experienced less frustration and more success when provided with prompts for the mind maps. In some cases, when the vocabulary definition was provided within the semantic mind map, students applied the word and moved on to the next reading level quicker than unprompted students.

If a student had a problem, the teacher noted the problem on the conference sheet. I then met individually with the student to show different ways to manage the problem until the student had enough knowledge to scaffold instruction.

After weeks of observing Interventions teachers, I realized that each one progressed through the direct instruction curriculum at a different pace. I created a revised template, in which I suggested that teachers teach three to four books per week. With this new goal, we noted that our students were improving on the progress monitor with even greater gains. We also realized that varying the lessons helped with learning, so we reminded teachers of multiple strategies to teach vocabulary and reading.

We modeled how to hold a book conference via video, which we streamed via Internet to all of our teachers. I also took pictures of teaches in their classrooms. When we saw that a teacher was implementing the program effectively, I snapped a picture and our principal posted the picture on the website.

Our principal continued to visit each classroom, and I continued to help in the library. Our Special Education teacher worked on progress monitoring and the Counselor made sure certain schedules were accurate.

As I reflected on our first year utilizing the program, I realized that teachers needed time not only to embrace RtI but also to learn the curriculum. It took patience and determination on the parts of everyone to implement such a complex program. We had come a long way, especially our teachers, who learned to:

CHAPTER SIX

- Pull leveled readers based on students' ZPD level,
- Conduct individual reading conferences with students,
- Use the SRA curriculum with reading comprehension strategies that I demonstrated, and
- Teach students word chunking skills.

When I informally interviewed teachers, they told me that students generally enjoyed the leveled readers. However, they wished they had entire class sets. Teachers also wanted to learn from each other; they wanted to discuss what other teachers were doing in order to revise and improve their own teaching strategies. It became apparent that in the following year we needed to teach the teachers: 1) how to do a fluency assessment within the leveled reading curriculum, and 2) how to do a Running Record with a leveled reader or an Accelerated Reader book, within the student's ZPD level, revised for the middle or high school student. We also needed to continue demonstrating comprehension strategies for the teachers and students.

Sharing an Intervention Case Study

One day, I learned that a student who tested into an Advanced Biology class was having reading difficulty. She scored +30 on her ISTEP Test. On the first MAZE assessment, she scored a 20, which did not meet the goal. Her ZPD range was 3.3-5.2 (grade level). This seventh grade student performed at two grade levels below standard. As the weeks passed into a month, she repeatedly approached me with tears streaming down her face. She consistently failed AR quizzes, and I had to modify her class tests because she did not comprehend what she was reading. I felt extremely sad watching her struggles and wondered what I could do to help.

Because she was in Advanced Science, she was in an Extensions class; however, this class was not meeting her reading needs. The parents were adamant and argued that she did not need help. To support the student, I created a file that she could use during Extensions class. In this file, I put developmentally appropriate books and reading passages to accelerate her reading comprehension. The Biology teacher administered the curriculum in a private way. Eventually, the mother saw her daughter's need and asked what she could do. I told her that we could move the student to an Interventions class; however, the mother continued to disagree. I recommended a tutoring program, and the mother liked the idea. Because we had data and observational records to support our intervention, this student received "hidden" help at school and tutoring at home. The student's integrity was preserved.

From this situation, I learned the importance of our RtI work. This student managed her classes but was not learning to comprehend text. The student's progress amazed me because she did what she needed to do, and she was successful. We soon discovered there were other students in our classrooms just like this one, and RtI provided a way for us to find gifted students with reading deficits in our advanced classes and empower teachers to meet their needs.

Training and Modeling for Extensions Classes

After working with the Interventions teachers for several months, I started visiting the classrooms of the Extensions teachers.

CHAPTER SIX

Teachers were engaged in book conferences and supplemental activities, such as EF Skills and Brain Gym, which were recommended by our Special Education teacher.

One Extensions teacher, Andy Wallace, approached me about adding a Book Club Discussion to his class. Book Club Discussions are easy to administer when everyone reads the same book, but I created a model for Andy's class to use for students who were all reading different books. In order to prepare for a Book Club Discussion, Andy and I conferred with individual students. We asked the students to list themes in their reading journals. For example, if a student was reading Three Cups of Tea by Greg Mortenson, the student might identify the theme as helpfulness. The student would then explain why he or she chose that theme and give an anecdote from the book. At that point, the student would lead the entire class in a question and challenge the class to connect helpfulness to their own books. The students loved these discussions!

Andy and I also asked the students to bring snacks to Book Club Discussions. Each student brought one food snack and a 20-ounce drink. They loved this component of the Book Club Discussion Day. Relaxing, eating, and talking about books in an informal way fostered a new love of reading and discussing books for these Extensions students.

Since our Book Club Discussions, Andy has continued to work with his students by creating games with SAT words. He has used many strategies, such as Stu's Quiz Boxes, which can be found online at http://quizboxes.com. Andy even led our entire faculty in a lesson on this quiz game. The website is a free resource anyone can use to create a vocabulary game for their students. Teachers like Andy inspired our entire RtI team to keep growing and keep learning.

Sharing Personal Reflections

RtI has become a thread that ties our school together, uniting teachers, students, and families. Teachers now have a path to impact students in a meaningful way and families have data to better understand their child's strengths and needs.

I remember when one of our veteran teachers sent me an e-mail at the beginning of the third month of the implementation process. The e-mail read:

> "I want you to know how wonderful the Interventions program is. I know you have been responsible for so much, without any extra time or compensation. In my 23 years at YMS, this is the most exciting thing we have ever done to REALLY make a difference in the education of a child. Thank you." –Marcia Losco, Social Studies

With this encouraging feedback, I realized that through RtI, our committed teachers were making a positive difference in the individual reading lives of each and every one of our students. RtI was providing a platform for instruction and a time to conference, encourage, and care for individual students. If the classroom teachers truly believe in meeting the needs of all students, then RtI will be a successful tool in your building, just as it was in ours.

CHAPTER SIX

Quick Chapter Review

This chapter equips the classroom teacher to do the following:
- Organize Interventions and Extensions Curriculum.
- Use your library to support reading instruction.
- Start a daily routine with a leveled reader curriculum.
- Help a student find a book at their independent reading level.
- Conference with students about books.

RECOLLECTIONS & REFLECTIONS
Chapter 6: RtI from a Teacher's Perspective

1. After you finish the chapter, close the book and write down 3 words or phrases that immediately come to mind.

2. Write down two helpful pieces of information you learned.

3. Write down one question that you still have.

4. Write down one way that this chapter has changed your thinking about RtI.

5. Write down any ideas you have for how you might implement something from this chapter.

CHAPTER SIX

6. Write down a significant "ah-ha" moment you experienced while reading this chapter (if any).

7. Describe something from your professional experience that came to mind as you worked with the ideas in this chapter.

8. Write down any resources from the chapter, your discussions, or personal web surfing that would help in implementing RtI in your school.

9. Is the goal that you identified at the beginning of this experience still the same? If not, explain why it changed and then write down your new goal.

CHAPTER SEVEN
SCHEDULING RTI

Katie Preston
Counselor

"I think Interventions class is awesome. You get to read your favorite books and talk about them." – Seventh Grade Boy

RtI From a Counselor's Perspective

I went to my first RtI conference in November 2007. Before attending this conference, I had only heard the term "RtI." I was not familiar with the definition of RtI or the kind of work it would take for a school to implement the process. The conference was called "The Nuts and Bolts of Response to Intervention." The speakers, Dr. Jim Surber and Marc Sgro, were very informative. I learned the definition of RtI, the key features involved in the process, as well as specific interventions to use for RtI.

After learning the basic components of RtI, I wondered about the role of a counselor. I sent out a question to my fellow counselors on our listserv. I asked how other middle schools were implementing RtI and what role school counselors were playing in RtI. I received very few responses and, out of the responses I did receive, most of them were asking the same question I was. Responses included:

> "We're working on it, but with middle school it is more difficult than with our elementary students…" and "I would love the information you receive as well. I am working on things for next year and using an [RtI] basis for dealing with 'F' lists at our school. My school does not use [RtI]."

Almost a year later, I attended one of our School Counseling Regional Meetings, held by the Indiana Department of Education in October 2008. One of the breakout sessions was on RtI. I was hoping this presentation would clarify the role of the counselor, but it did not. I have learned, however, that it is important for the school counselor to be a part of the RtI team, though that role will depend on the needs of the school. You may have several roles, or just one or two.

After I joined the RtI team in our building, we questioned, "When in the school day are we going to implement RtI?" This question led me to my major role in the RtI process: creating the master schedule.

Creating the Master Schedule

As the only Guidance Counselor at YMS, one of my many duties was to create the Master Schedule each year for our building. It is the least favorite part of my job; however, I knew it was a key to successful implementation of RtI for YMS because it impacts everyone in the school. To add a new program and then find a time slot for that program during the school day was a difficult task. Most teachers already had multiple duties, so I quickly realized that we did not have enough teachers or places in our building to execute the multiple periods of instruction which the RtI process demanded for Tier 2 and Tier 3 students.

Our school runs an eight-period day, with 40 minutes for each class period. We have five core classes: Math, Language Arts, Reading, Social Studies, and Science. Our students receive two Encore classes such as Physical Education, Art, Health, Family Consumer Sciences, or Computers. Our Encore classes rotate every nine weeks, giving our students the opportunity to experience all classes. Our eighth period has traditionally been a student elective period. Students select one course such as: Psychology, Current Events, Jazz Band, Musical Productions, Challenge of the Mind, or a study hall. In the past few years, we have offered a Resource Study Hall (RSH) for students who qualified through an IEP (Individualized Education Plan) for additional support services. If a student was in RSH, then he or she could only experience one Encore class. To complicate matters, if a student needed an RSH and elected to take Band, he or she would miss out on all other Encore opportunities. Throughout our continuing discussions about the best ways to serve our students in Tier 2 or Tier 3, we discovered another issue. In our current schedule, if a student needed an RSH but was placed in Tier 2 or Tier 3, the student would not be able to take Band.

In the RtI conferences I attended, several schools talked about pulling students from their "specials" or what we termed Encore classes. In fact, when I asked fellow counselors on the listserv how they were meeting RtI objectives in middle school classrooms, the response was that students missed out on an elective. I really wanted that to be a last resort. I worked with several students who struggled with reading or math yet excelled in music, art, or computers. These students would be the ones who would miss out on Encore classes, yet I knew many of them already struggled with their confidence in academics.

Our RtI team discussed this issue at length. We were all in agreement that we did not want our students to miss an Encore class. One of my favorite scheduling tools has been a book entitled, Making Creative Schedules Work. I was fortunate enough to attend a seminar with the authors of this book, Elliot Merenbloom and Barbara Kalina. One of Elliot's key strategies toward making a successful schedule is to "move the variables." This phrase transitioned the focus of our schedule.

Our school was fortunate because we already had an existing elective period built into the end of our school day. We typically used this time for ISTEP Remediation, study hall, and various other elective courses, so instead of giving students a choice for eighth period, we placed them in a class based upon their reading level because reading was our RtI focus. We thought we could group those students who placed in Tier 2 and Tier 3 into smaller classes according to students' needs. Those students in Tier 1 would be in much larger class sizes, since they did not need the direct instruction. All classes would meet every day for 40 minutes. The students that needed Tier 3 instruction, or the "triple dip," would attend their General Education Reading class, receive direct instruction during eighth period, and get the third intervention of direct instruction during one Encore class time. In creating the schedule this way, the students who needed the most intervention would still be able to have one Encore class in their day. This change would allow students in Tier 3 to take

CHAPTER SEVEN

Band, Computers, Art, or Health. The students that placed in Tier 2 and needed the "double dip" would attend their General Education Reading class and receive the direct instruction during eighth period. This process allowed students in Tier 2 to attend two Encore classes. My principal and I were thrilled at integrating interventions into our day, while not compromising the middle school concept of exploring other classes. Our students who needed the "triple dip" would still be able to experience one of our Encore classes and the students who needed the "double dip" would get both Encores. We wanted students to understand that the Interventions class was not an "add on" or an elective class, but an important part of the day.

At first, the class was called "Interventions," even though we realized that it was not truly an intervention for all students. As the school year approached, my principal renamed the class to "Interventions and Extensions." The name change may not seem remarkable; however, it was dramatic and transforming for our school because it conveyed the overall meaning of this class. We wanted to meet the needs of all students, so we would intervene for those students who needed it but also challenge the students who were reading at or above grade level to read at higher levels.

At the start of the school year, the Leadership Team met again with each building's RtI team in our corporation. It was important for our corporation to communicate between grade levels and buildings to make sure we all had continuity and fluidity. We discussed how students in each building were receiving the direct instruction they needed in Tier 2 and Tier 3. We also discussed how we were going to communicate RtI to our parents and families. (See Appendix G for a sample master schedule.)

Quick Chapter Review

This chapter explains the following:

- RtI from a counselor's perspective
- Creating the master schedule

RECOLLECTIONS & REFLECTIONS
Chapter 7: Scheduling RtI

1. After you finish the chapter, close the book and write down 3 words or phrases that immediately come to mind.

2. Write down two helpful pieces of information you learned.

3. Write down one question that you still have.

4. Write down one way that this chapter has changed your thinking about RtI.

5. Write down any ideas you have for how you might implement something from this chapter.

6. Write down a significant "ah-ha" moment you experienced while reading this chapter (if any).

7. Describe something from your professional experience that came to mind as you worked with the ideas in this chapter.

8. Write down any resources from the chapter, your discussions, or personal web surfing that would help in implementing RtI in your school.

9. Is the goal that you identified at the beginning of this experience still the same? If not, explain why it changed and then write down your new goal.

CHAPTER EIGHT
FAMILY PARTNERSHIP

Katie Preston
Counselor

"My Interventions and Extensions class has given me time to learn and to read. I have learned how to read a passage. I have been given time to complete a book…I also have time to gather my thoughts and think about what I am reading…"

– Seventh Grade Girl

Parents are important stakeholders to their children's education (Merenbloom & Kalina, 2007). Our Leadership Team knew that communication was going to be something we had to handle well from the start. We wanted parents to understand and support our Interventions and Extensions class. In order for parents to understand the intervention process, they first needed to learn what YMS was doing in the classroom.

Communication

Before school starts each year, students and parents come and register, as well as receive students' schedules. The RtI Leadership

Team designated registration as the starting point for the communication process with parents. We wanted parents to understand RtI and their student's placement in an Interventions or an Extensions class. As our front office staff prepared the packets to mail home for registration, we included a brochure about RtI. The original document, which detailed the definition and overall premise of RtI, was posted on the Indiana Department of Education's website (IDOE, 2009), but we revised it to meet the needs of our school. When the parents and students came to register, each family received another copy of the brochure.

As I handed out schedules and explained the new Interventions and Extensions class, I fielded many questions: "What is this class?" "Another Reading class?" "Will there be homework involved?" There were also complaints: "I cannot believe we don't have study halls!" "Now, there will not be enough time to complete our homework." "I am a good reader, and I do not need another reading class!" I even had some parents voice their frustration over losing the study halls. Parental concern revolved around their student's active involvement in extracurricular activities. Some parents wanted students to complete homework at school. I could understand their concerns and knew this year would have to be an adjustment period. As Merenbloom and Kalina state, "Study halls should be reduced, if not eliminated, in the middle grades" (2007). In the end, we hoped parents would discover the new Interventions or Extensions class would benefit their students in ways a study hall never could.

Letters

Indiana's Article 7 provided some guidelines on how to notify parents of a student's placement in a Tier.

CHAPTER EIGHT

> 511 IAC 7-40-2 (f): Parent of a student who participates in…(RtI process) must be provided with written notification when a student requires an intervention that is not provided to all students in the general education classroom (IDOE, 2009).

For the students in Tier 2 and Tier 3, we mailed home a letter indicating the direct services their student would be receiving. (See Appendices H and I for sample letters.)

Phone Calls

During the first three weeks of school, I fielded questions every day from parents about this new RtI class. I would always remind them about the RtI brochure which they received in the mail and at registration. Many had forgotten but some remembered. The main question was, "How did my child place in a Tier?" and "What are you doing in this class?" After I took a few minutes to explain our process, the MAZE test, EF skills, and leveled readers, most parents supported the proposed changes. I was surprised to discover that out of the seventy-six students placed in Tier 2, I only had one parent who questioned their child's placement. The Tier 2 parents seemed to be the most excited and encouraged that their student would be receiving extra support. One of the parents called me and said,

> "I am so glad you are having this class. My daughter has always struggled with reading comprehension. I have worried about how she will do in high school with being able to understand the text. I feel hopeful about what you are doing and how this will help in the future!"

The Red Folder

Another step in our communication process is what we have affectionately called the "Red Folder." The Red Folder contains data collected for those students who may possibly need special services. Our previous Special Education Director came up with this system to efficiently gather the data we needed to make decisions in case conferences about students needing services. The Red Folder is literally a red folder containing several documents to detail a student's progress, such as MAZE scores, ISTEP scores, current grades, benchmark tests, any accommodations currently provided, and all implemented intervention strategies.

Before RtI, when a parent called and requested testing, we had several days to test. As we waited, we held a conference and tried to use interventions in the general education classroom to help the students while we waited for the testing results. Now, when a parent requests testing, we still test; however, during the waiting period, we have our eighth period Interventions class that provides direct instruction (research based interventions), separate from the general education class. The Red Folder is created to collect student data from the time interventions began to the day of the parent conference to decide eligibility for special services. During this time, the student's progress during the intervention and direct instruction is measured. If the student is not currently in a Tier 2 class, we begin to progress monitor. We progress monitor through the MAZE every two weeks to document the student's growth.

In addition, when a teacher observes a student who is not successful in the classroom and for whom general classroom interventions are not effective, the teacher contacts me to begin

CHAPTER EIGHT

gathering data. If this student was not already in Tier 2, we would begin a progress monitor every two weeks. Knowing that all of our students are in an Interventions or Extensions class, we are assured that they are all receiving some sort of extra attention in reading comprehension.

In October 2009, I attended my first Red Folder meeting. In this case, parents requested testing for students' learning disabilities in September 2009. When the parents signed the request for testing, the Special Education Coordinator notified me, and I started the Red Folder on the student.

One particular student was in a Tier 2 class and had received direct instruction since August 2009. He was being progress monitored every two weeks. At the initial meeting, the extended RtI team was present to discuss the student's data. Our extended RtI team included the school psychologist, a Special Education teacher, the principal, school counselor, and Reading teacher. This extended RtI team came to the Red Folder conference and helped to determine if a student qualified for special services. The student's parents were not asked to attend this initial meeting. I shared the data in the Red Folder, the school psychologist shared the student's test results, and the student's Interventions teacher discussed his progress with the leveled readers. It was encouraging for all of us to see the consistency of the data and this student's progress. The next step was to share the Red Folder data with the parents. The extended RtI team met with the student's parents the next week. The team shared the results from the testing, the Red Folder, and Interventions class with the parents, who were encouraged when they saw the data and the positive growth in their child. They agreed the interventions currently in place were effective. The decision was made by the RtI team and the parents to keep the student in Tier 2 and continue progress monitoring every two weeks. The parents left the meeting expressing their gratitude for all we were doing to improve their son's reading comprehension. The parents commented: "We feel that this is the first 'real' reading remediation [our eighth grader] has had in middle school."

Since my first Red Folder meeting, I have experienced two other Red Folder meetings. The results were very similar to the first one. The data was comprehensive, the interventions were appropriate, and the parents were impressed with the RtI process. We have found that in communicating to parents the process of RtI, they have been supportive and pleased with the results.

Quick Chapter Review

This chapter highlights the partnership between the school and the family through the following methods of communication:

- Letters
- Phone calls
- The Red Folder

RECOLLECTIONS & REFLECTIONS
Chapter 8: Family Partnership

1. After you finish the chapter, close the book and write down 3 words or phrases that immediately come to mind.

2. Write down two helpful pieces of information you learned.

3. Write down one question that you still have.

4. Write down one way that this chapter has changed your thinking about RtI.

5. Write down any ideas you have for how you might implement something from this chapter.

6. Write down a significant "ah-ha" moment you experienced while reading this chapter (if any).

7. Describe something from your professional experience that came to mind as you worked with the ideas in this chapter.

8. Write down any resources from the chapter, your discussions, or personal web surfing that would help in implementing RtI in your school.

9. Is the goal that you identified at the beginning of this experience still the same? If not, explain why it changed and then write down your new goal.

CHAPTER NINE
CONCLUDING THOUGHTS

Amy Carney-Heath
Reading Specialist & Teacher

"RtI is vital because it brings spotlight to those in need, it is beneficial because it offers growth for every student regardless of ability level. My daughter was a good reader who read sometimes and now she is an excellent reader who won't go to bed at night because her book is so compelling." – Parent

Over the course of a year, our middle school has implemented a successful RtI reading curriculum. RtI created a facet in our curriculum to serve students at their individual reading levels. At the beginning of the year, we had 76 students who entered a reading-focused Interventions class in Tier 2 or Tier 3. After many meetings with educational professionals and parents, our RtI team learned to focus on data and results. Even if our hearts desired for students to receive additional instruction, we realized that we could not go with our hearts. We made decisions based on data, so our decisions would be consistent. If students earned five consecutive points above the Aimline, we moved them from Tier 2 and progress monitored students as they continued with the core curriculum. By the end of April, over 30 students met benchmark goals as they went through this process. The remaining students continued to receive Tier 2 instruction.

RtI equipped every teacher in our building to understand the multiple facets of reading instruction. Each teacher learned how to have a book conference with a student, how to examine data from the MAZE and STAR assessments, how to help a student choose a book at his or her independent reading level, how to increase reading skills regardless of current reading level, and how to implement the SRA curriculum. RtI provided a platform for our teachers to match assessment to curriculum.

Next year, with the help of our superintendent, administrators, and teachers, we hope to integrate a Tier 2 and Tier 3 for math. Like with reading, we will conduct a universal screen for math, as well as provide a curriculum with direct instruction. We will then address behavior skills in the same manner the following year.

As we continue to learn and grow with this process, we continue to be amazed with its results. We wish you well on your journey of *Implementing RTI Successfully in Your Middle/High School*.

REFERENCES

Bear, D., Invernizzi, M., Templeton, S., & Johnston, F. (2007). *Words Their Way*. Salt Lake City, Utah: Pearson.

Benner, R. (2008). Response to Intervention (RTI) within the context of Data-based Decision Making. *Indiana Response to Intervention* (p. 10). Indianapolis: NEA IDEA Resource Cadre.

Casey, Elliot, & Prasse (2008). RTI Action Network, National Online Forum. *Are You Ready for RTI?* www.rtinetwork.org

Clay, M. (1993). *An Observation Survey: Of Early Literacy Achievement*. Westport, CT: Greenwood Press.

Clay, M. (2000). *Running Records for Classroom Teachers*. Portsmouth, NH: Heinemann Educational Books.

Cox, D. A. (2008). *No Mind Left Behind: Understanding and Fostering Executive Control–The Eight Essential Brain Skills Every Child Needs to Thrive*. New York City, NY: Penguin Group.

Cunningham, P., & Hall, D. (2006). *Big Blocks Grades 4-8*. New York, NY: Carson-Dellosa Publishing.

Dennison, P. E., & Dennison, G. E. (1986). *Brain Gym*. Ventura: Edu-Kinesthetics, Inc.

Dickman, G. E. (2006). *RTI and Reading: REsponse to Intervention in a Nutshell*. Baltimore, Maryland: The International Dyslexia Association.

Education NASP. (2008). Response to Intervention Blueprints for Implementation. *Indiana Department of Education Response to Intervention Conference* (p. 9). Alexandria, VA: National Association of State Directors of Special Education.

Fountas, I., & Pinnel, G. (2008). *When Readers Struggle*. Portsmouth, NH: Heinemann Educational Books.

Hall, T. (2002). *Differentiated instruction*. Wakefield, MA: CAST.www.cast.org/publications/ncac/ncac_diffinstruc.html

Hosp, M.K., Hosp, J. L., & Howell, K.W. (2007). *The ABCs of CBM*. New York City, NY: The Guilford Press.

Indiana Department of Education (2009). *Indiana's Response to Intervention*. www.doe.in.gove/indiana-rti/rti.html

International Reading Association (2005). *Response to Intervention*. www.reading.org.

International Reading Association (retrieved 2004). *Response to Intervention in the Individuals with Disabilities Act*. www.

reading.org. Written by Fiona James, Dec. 5, 2004. www.reading.org/downloads/resources.IDEA_RTI_report.pdf.

Jay, J. (2009). Leadership, Core Curriculum, and Fidelity. *Indiana's Response to Intervention Academy*. Indianapolis, IN: Indiana Department of Education.

Johnson, A.P., & Rasmussen, J.B. (1998). Classifying and Super Word Web: Two Strategies to Improve Productive Vocabulary. *Journal of Adolescent & Adult Literacy, 42*, 204-207.

Marcia R. Davidson, T. C. (2005). *Reading Fluency Monitor Benchmark.* Saint Paul, MN: Read Naturally, Inc.

Maxwell, J.C. (1995). *Developing the Leaders Around You.* Nashville, TN: Thomas Nelson

Maxwell, J.C. (2009). *How Successful People Think.* Nashville, TN: Center Street Publishing.

Merenbloom, E., & Kalina, B. (2007). *Making Creative Schedules Work.* Thousand Oaks, CA: Corwin Press.

Merenbloom, E., & Kalina, B. (2009, November 6). Workshop. Presented at the National Middle School Association Conference, Indianapolis.

Palenchar, L., & Boyer, L. (2008). Response to Intervention: Implementation of a Statewide System. *Rural Special Education Quarterly*, 27 (4): 18-26.

Rathvon, N. (2008). *Effective School Interventions.* New York City, NY: The Guilford Press.

Reid, R. (2009). Universal Screening and Progress Monitoring. *Indiana's Response to Intervention Academy* (p. 4). Indianapolis, IN: Indiana Department of Education.

Robb, L. (2008). *Differentiating Reading Instruction.* New York, NY: Great Source Education Group.

Robb, L. (2010). *Teaching Reading in the Middle School.* New York, NY: Great Source Education Group.

RTI Action Network National Online Forum (2008). *Are you ready for RTI?* rtinetwork.org

Samuels, C. (2009). High Schools Try Out RTI. *Education Week*, 28 (19): 20-22.

Shores, C.F., & Chester, K.B. (2008). *Using RTI for School Improvement: Raising Every Student's Achievement Scores.* Thousand Oaks, CA: Corwin Press.

SRA Teacher's Guide Leveled Reader Intervention. (2008). SRA/McGraw-Hill.

Surber, J., & Sgro, M. (2007, November 14). Workshop. The Nuts and Bolts of Response to Intervention, Indianapolis.

Tomlinson, C. (2005). *How to Differentiate Instruction in Mixed-Ability Classrooms.* Upper Saddle River, NJ: Pearson.

Wright, J. (2009). *jim@jimwrightonline.* Retrieved February 13, 2010, from Intervention Central: www.interventioncentral.org.

Wooden, J., & Jamison, S. (2005). *Wooden on Leadership.* New

York, NY: McGraw-Hill.

Yuri Kashima, K., Scheleich, B., & Spradlin, T. (2009). *The Core Components of RTI: A Closer Look at Evidence-based Core Curriculum, Assessment and Progress Monitoring, and Data-Based Decision Making.* Bloomington, IN: Center for Evaluation and Education Policy.

Zillich, J. L. (2009). Assessment and Progress Monitoring Within the Context of Response to Intervention. *National Association of School Psychologists* (p. 23). Indianapolis, IN: IDEA Partnership.

ADDITIONAL RESOURCES

Allington, R. L. (2008). *What Really Matters in Response to Intervention: Research-based Designs.* Upper Saddle River, N. J.: Allyn & Bacon.

Allington, R., & Walmsley, S. (2007). *No Quick Fix: Rethinking Literacy Programs in America's Elementary Schools, The RTI Edition.* New York: Teachers College Press & International Reading Association.

Beech, L. (2006). *Context Clues & Figurative Language.* New York, NY: Scholastic.

Beech, L. (2006). *Inferences and Drawing Conclusions.* New York, NY: Scholastic.

Beech, L. (2006). *Main Ideas & Summarizing.* New York, NY: Scholastic.

Fogarty, R. & Pete, B. (December 2009/January 2010). *Professional learning 101: A syllabus of seven.* The Kappan, 91(4), 32-34.

Howard, M. (2009). *RTI From All Sides: What Every Teacher Needs to Know.* Portsmouth, N. H.: Heinemann.

Nellis, L. (2009). *Project for Responsive Educational Systems.* Terre Haute, IN: Indiana State University.

Network: Reading, Q. T. (2006). *A Model Secondary (6-12) Plan for Reading Intervention and Development.* Minnesota: Minnesota Department of Education.

Owocki, G. (2010) *The RTI Daily Planning Book, K-6: Tools and Strategies for Collecting and Assessing Reading Data & Targeted Follow-Up Instruction.* Portsmouth, N. H.: Heinemann.

Snobarger, A. (2008, October 6). Presentation. School Counselor Regional Workshop, Indianapolis.

Staff, M. A. (2009). MacArthur RTI Handbook. *Indiana's Response to Intervention Academy* (p. 6). Cedar Lake, IN: MacArthur Elementary.

Stecker, P., Fuchs, D., & Fuchs, L. (2008). Progress Monitoring as Essential Practice Within Response to Intervention. *Rural Special Education Quarterly*, 27 (4): 10-17.

APPENDICES

Appendix A: Reading Improvement Report for 2009 to 2010 School Year

Grade 7 - Compared to Yorktown Middle School Maze Comprehension

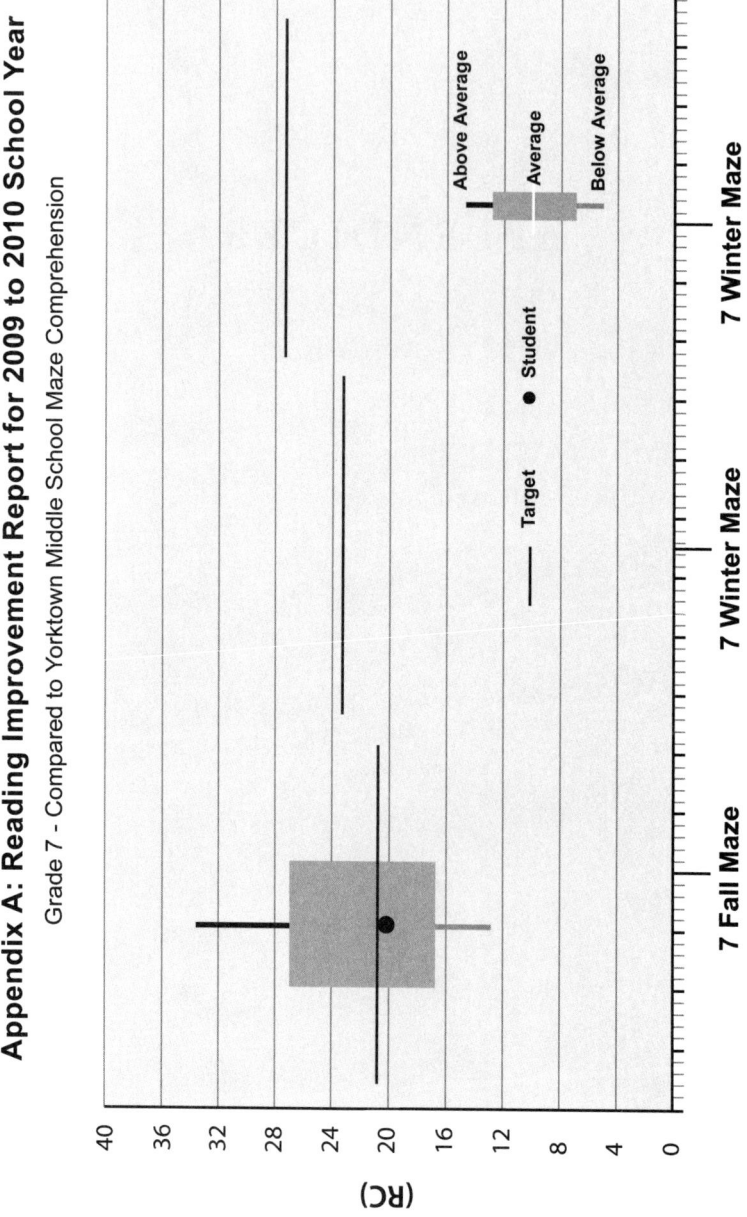

132

Benchmark Comparison: Yorktown Middle School

Outcome Measure	Year	Grade	Fall	Winter	Spring	Skill Level	Instructional Recommendation
MAZE Comprehension (MAZE)	2008-2010	7	20.0			Average	Continue Current Program (Yorktown Middle School Fall percentiles)

Copyright © 2008 by NSA Pearson, Inc. All Rights Reserved. Patent No. 7,311.62

Appendix B: Progress Monitoring Improvement Report
08/27/2009 to 05/14/2010 - Grade 8 Maze Comprehension

Goal Statement: *In 37.1 weeks, _____ will achieve 26 Responses Correct with 0 Errors from grade 8 MAZE - Comprehension. The rate of improvement should be 0.43 Responses Correct per week. The current average rate of improvement is 0.62 Responses Correct per week.*

Date	08/27 *	10/29	11/12	12/03	12/17	01/22	02/04
Corrects	10	21	15	24	22	20	28
Errors	3	1	5	2	1	2	3
Goal/Trend ROI	0.43/0.62						

* Data from 8/27 are baseline/goals sessions.
Goal Changes & Intervention Descriptions:
8/27/2009: (Baseline Corrects = 10; Goal Corrects = 26)
Copyright © 2010 by NCS Pearson, Inc.

Appendix B Continued: Progress Monitoring Improvement Graph

135

Appendix C: Data Utilized for Decision Rules (Grade 8)

8th grade	Universal screen current (MAZE)	Tier from Spring US (DIBELS)	ISTEP Language Arts	STAR ZPD
Student 1	Well below avg	1	Pass	3.5-5.5
2	Well below avg	1	Did not pass	2.8-4.1
3	Below average	1	Did not pass	3.7
4	Average	1	Pass	3.5
(Spcd) 5	Well below avg	1	Pass	4.5-8.0
6	Well below avg	1	Pass	3.6-5.6
7	Well below avg	1	Did not pass	3.6-5.6
8	Average	1	Did not pass	3.9-5.9
9	Well below avg	1	Did not pass	3.6-5.6
(ESL) 10	Below average	1	Did not pass	3.1-4.8
11	Average	1	Did not pass	2.9-4.3
12	Average	1	Did not pass	3.8-5.9

Appendix D: Data Utilized for Decision Rules (Grade 7)

7th grade	Universal screen current (MAZE)	Tier from Spring US (DIBELS)	ISTEP Language Arts	STAR ZPD
Student 1	Below average	1	Pass	3.7-5.7
2	Below average	1	Pass	3.9-5.9
(ESL) 3	Below average	1	Pass	3.5
4	Well below avg	1	Did not pass	3.2-5.1
(Autism) 5	Well below avg	1	Pass	
6	Well below avg	1	Did not pass	3.7-5.7
7	Average	1	Did not pass	3.4-5.4
8	Average	1	Did not pass	3.2-5.1
9	Below average	1	Did not pass	4.4-7.4
10	Below average	1	Did not pass	4.1-6.3
(Spced) 11	Average	1	Did not pass	3.5-5.5
12	Average	1	Did not pass	4.1-6.3
13	Average	1	Did not pass	1.2-2.8
14	Average	1	Did not pass	3.4-4.2

Appendix E: Reading Log & Reading Strategies

NAME			
DATE	TITLE/AUTHOR	**Reflections** *How did you connect with the book that you are reading? What did you like about your book? What would you change about your book?*	Page to page

Appendix E Continued: READING STRATEGIES

Before Reading *These strategies activate past knowledge and experiences.*	Brainstorm Categorize Predict Pre-teach vocabulary	Preview, Skim Pose questions Fast-write What do I know?	Visualize KWL Charts Guess/Check Vocab Support
During Reading *These strategies enable students to make personal connections, visualize, identify parts that confuse, monitor understanding, and recall information.*	Make personal connections Use prior knowledge Predict Support Adjust or confirm	Pose questions Identify confusing parts Visualize Self-monitor	Summarize Synthesize Reread Use context clues Infer
After Reading *These strategies progress past the knowledge level, deepen understanding and engagement of text, and can create connections to other texts.*	Skim Reread Question Visualize the text Evaluate the text Compare/Contrast	Adjust Predictions State theme Note-taking Summarize Cause/Effect	Infer Conclude Reflect through Talking, Writing, or Drawing

Appendix F

VOCABULARY GUESS & CHECK

Vocabulary Word	Guess	Check
Teachers listed the vocabulary words in the boxes before they copied this template. The teacher asked the students if there were any words that the student could not pronounce and pronounced the words with the students.	Students recorded their guesses to the meaning of vocabulary words here. Students were also encouraged to draw pictures of the meaning of the words.	How did you connect with the book that you are reading? What did you like about your book? What would you change about your book?

Infer *(example)*

Evaluate *(example)*

Appendix G: Sample Master Schedule

Period 1	Period 2	Period 3	Period 4	Period 5	Period 5/L	Period 6	Period 7	Period 8
Alg. 7	Prep	M7	Pre-Alg 7	M7	LU	M7	Pre-Alg 7	I & E
Read 7	Prep	Read 7	Read 7	Read 7	LU	A. Read. 7	Read. 7	Rdg Specialist
SS 7	SS7	SS 7	SS 7	SS 7	LU	Prep	SS 7	I & E
Sci 7	Sci 7	Prep	Sci 7	Sci 7	LU	Sci 7	A.Sci 7	A. Sci-Lab
L/A 7	A. LA 7	L/A 7	Prep	LA 7	LU	LA 7	LA 7	I & E
LA 8	L/A 8	LA 7	LA 7	Prep	LU	L/A 7	L/A 7	I & E
M 7	M 7	Prep	Alg. 8	LU	Pre-Alg 8	Alg. 8	M 7	I & E
SS 8	Prep	SS 7	SS 7	LU	SS 8	SS 7	SS 8	I & E
Sci 7	Sci 7	Sci 8	Prep	Sci 7	LU	Sci 8	Sci 7	I & E
Read 7	Read 7	Read. 7	Read. 7	LU	Read. 8	Prep	Read 8	PUB
Pre-Alg 8	Pre-Alg 8	Pre-Alg 8	Prep	LU	Geo. 8	Pre-Alg 8	Pre-Alg 8	I & E
A. LA 8	LA 8	Prep	LA 8	LU	LA 8	LA 8	LA 8	I & E
SS 8	SS 8	SS 8	SS 8	SS 8	SS 8	Prep	SS 8	I & E
Sci 8	Sci 8	Sci 8	Prep	LU	Sci 8	Sci 8	BIO	BIO Lab
Read 8	Read 8	A. Read. 8	Read. 8	LU	Prep	Read. 8	Read. 8	I & E

Appendix H: Tier 2 Letter to Parents

Dear Parent/Guardian,

As part of our ongoing commitment to meet the needs of all students, we have developed initiatives to provide additional support to help students strengthen fundamental skills. Students are recommended for additional supports based on their scores on universal screening measurements. Based on your student's performance, he/she will receive instruction in addition to the instruction in his/her classroom; this additional instruction is not generally provided to all students in the classroom but it is scientific, research or evidence based and is being provided with the intention of increasing your student's rate of learning.

We hope that the plan is successful. However, if after a designated period of time, we do not see evidence that your student is making adequate progress based on regular progress monitoring, we will meet with you to determine an individualized plan of support for your student. During the implementation of the plan, we will continue to monitor your student's progress. If your student does not make adequate progress, we may initiate a request for an educational evaluation.

It is your right to request an educational evaluation at any time. The information from the education evaluation will be used in conjunction with the data collected during the intervention process in the consideration of eligibility for special education and related services.

If you would like more information about the intervention plan developed for your student or if you wish to request an educational evaluation, please contact your student's teacher or principal.

Sincerely,

Heath Dudley
Principal

Appendix I: Tier 3 Letter to Parents

Dear Parent,

It has been determined that your child will participate in intervention that is not generally provided to all students in the classroom. This process will include the assessment of your child's response to scientific, research-based intervention with the intention of increasing your child's rate of learning to grade level.

We hope that this plan is successful. However, if your child has not made adequate progress after the designated period of time, we may initiate a request for an educational evaluation to determine if your child is eligible for special education and related services. To initiate this request, we will send you a notice describing the evaluation process and ask for your written consent.

Once you consent to the evaluation and the evaluation is complete, we will invite you to join the school personnel in a case conference committee meeting where we will review the evaluation results and determine if your child is eligible for special education and related services. The evaluation will be conducted and the case conference committee will meet within 20 school days of the date the school receives your written consent.

At any time, it is your right to request an educational evaluation which will produce information used in the consideration of eligibility for special education and related services. Within 10 school days of your request, we will provide you with a notice of evaluation which will outline the evaluation procedures. The evaluation will be conducted and the case conference committee will meet within 50 school days of the date the school receives your consent to this notice.

Please contact your child's teacher or building administrator if you wish to request such an evaluation.

Sincerely,

Heath Dudley
Principal

> # ABOUT THE AUTHORS

AMY CARNEY HEATH

Reading Specialist & Teacher

Mrs. Amy Carney Heath earned her Bachelor's degree in Elementary/Middle Education in 1997 from Guilford College, Greensboro, North Carolina. She earned a Gifted and Talented License in 2002 and was chosen to pilot USTARS Gifted and Talented Program for Dr. Mary Ruth Coleman, UNC Chapel Hill. In 2008, she earned her Master of Arts degree in Education, with a Reading Specialist License, from Ball State University in Muncie, Indiana. In addition to her current responsibilities at YMS as the Reading teacher, Amy is the co-chair for the Gifted Program for the Mount Pleasant School Corporation and a consultant/teacher for the accelerated Saturday and summer outreach programs, sponsored by the Indiana Academy for Science, Mathematics, and Humanities, Muncie, Indiana.

Amy's passion is most evident when she talks of her summers with orphans and widows in Kenya, where she serves as a reading consultant and early literacy curriculum designer for the Village Project Africa in Kenya. Frustrated with the rote methods of instruction currently employed in Kenya, Amy is dedicated to equipping eager Kenyan educators with effective strategies to teach early literacy.

Amy's heart for enabling children to read successfully continues to energize her as she inspires and mentors educators around the world.

Amy resides in Muncie, Indiana with her new husband, Kevin Heath.

HEATH DUDLEY

School Principal

Mr. Heath Dudley's professional training took place at Ball State University located in Muncie, Indiana. He graduated with a Bachelor of Science degree in Elementary Education in 1999 and completed his Masters of Arts in Educational Administration and Supervision in 2004.

Heath was awarded the honorable distinction of Middle School Principal of the Year for 2009 by the Indiana Association of School Principals District 6. In 2010, he completed the Indiana Principal's Leadership Academy.

Prior to being named principal, Heath served Yorktown Middle School students and families in the role of assistant principal and classroom teacher. The 2009-2010 school year marked Heath's eleventh year in public education, all of which have been at Yorktown Middle School.

Heath currently resides in Selma, Indiana with his wife, Jessica, of nine years and his three children. Heath and his family enjoy traveling, athletics, and spending time as a family.

JAN BROWN

Special Education Teacher & Behavioral Consultant

Mrs. Jan Brown received a Bachelor of Science in Elementary Education from Indiana University in 1983 and a Master of Science in Special Education from Ball State University in 1991. Jan has been teaching Special Education courses for 22 years. Jan's first position was in a residential setting for adolescent boys who had been expelled from public education. She spent eight years in Blackford County Schools in Indiana. While there, Jan taught in a mild-disabilities classroom for Kindergarten through fifth grade and secondary emotional disabilities for several years before becoming a teacher and behavior consultant with Yorktown Community Schools in 1997. Jan serves as part of the Yorktown corporation Autism team and is a teacher/trainer for Nonviolent Crisis Intervention. In 2009, she was awarded the Educator of the Month distinction by WLBC radio. She was also named Educator of the Year by INSOURCE for partnering with families of children with special needs.

Jan is a wife of 22 years. Her husband Kevin is a network and systems engineer with Accutech Systems. Jan's children are Kenneth, a junior in college, Thomas, a freshman in high school, and Katherine, a seventh grader. Jan and her family enjoy traveling, camping, music, and spending time together.

KATIE PRESTON

School Counselor

Mrs. Katie Preston graduated from Anderson University in 1996 with a Bachelor's Degree in Social Work. Katie worked at a women's homeless shelter as a case manager before taking time off to be a stay-at-home mom. She returned to work in 2002 as a hospice social worker at Saint John's Health System in Anderson, Indiana.

In 2004, Katie began classes at Ball State University, pursuing a Master's Degree in School Counseling, which she obtained in 2006. While attending BSU, she counseled high school juniors and seniors at the Indiana Academy. In July 2006, Katie was hired as the school counselor at Yorktown Middle School in Yorktown, Indiana. She is in her fourth year at YMS and enjoys her work with adolescent students.

Katie lives in Anderson, Indiana. She has been happily married to her wonderful husband, Dave, for over 15 years. Katie is the proud mom of two amazing sons, 13-year-old Jacob and 11-year-old Nathan.